The Spiritual Exercises
of St. Ignatius

IGNATIUS OF LOYOLA

The Spiritual Exercises *of* St. Ignatius

BASED ON STUDIES IN THE
LANGUAGE OF THE AUTOGRAPH

TRANSLATED BY
Louis J. Puhl, S. J.

PREFACE BY
Avery Dulles, S. J.

VINTAGE SPIRITUAL CLASSICS

VINTAGE BOOKS
A DIVISION OF RANDOM HOUSE, INC.
NEW YORK

A VINTAGE SPIRITUAL CLASSICS ORIGINAL, December 2000
FIRST EDITION
Editing and arrangement of the texts,
About the Vintage Spiritual Classics, Preface to the Vintage Spiritual
Classics Edition, Chronology of the Life of St. Ignatius of Loyola,
and Suggestions for Further Reading
Copyright © 2000 by Random House, Inc.

Library of Congress Cataloging-in-Publication Data
Vintage is a registered trademark and Vintage Spiritual Classics
and colophon are trademarks of Random House, Inc.

ISBN: 978-0-375-72492-3

www.randomhouse.com

Book design by Fritz Metsch

Printed in the United States of America

13

CONTENTS

*Indented numbers refer to sections, not book-page numbers. (Eds.)

*Refers to page numbers, not to section numbers.

A turn or shift of sorts is becoming evident in the reflections of men and women today on their life experiences. Not quite as adamantly secular and, perhaps, a little less insistent on material satisfactions, the reading public has recently developed a certain attraction to testimonies that human life is leavened by a Presence that blesses and sanctifies. Recovery, whether from addictions or personal traumas, illness, or even painful misalignments in human affairs, is evolving from the standard therapeutic goal of enhanced self-esteem. Many now seek a deeper healing that embraces the whole person, including the soul. Contemporary books provide accounts of the invisible assistance of angels. The laying on of hands in prayer has made an appearance at the hospital bedside. Guides for the spiritually perplexed have risen to the tops of best-seller lists. The darkest shadows of skepticism and unbelief, which have eclipsed the presence of the Divine in our rational age, are beginning to lighten and part.

If the power and presence of God are real and effective, what do they mean for human experience? What does He offer to men and women, and what does He ask in return? How do we recognize Him? Know Him? Respond to Him? God has a reputation for being both benevolent and wrathful. Which will He be for me and when? Can these aspects of the Divine somehow be reconciled? Where is God when I suffer? Can I lose Him? Is God truthful, and are His promises to be trusted?

Are we really as precious to God as we are to ourselves and our loved ones? Do His providence and amazing grace guide our faltering steps toward Him, even in spite of ourselves? Will God abandon us if the sin is serious enough, or if we have episodes of resistance and forgetfulness? These are fundamental questions any person might address to God during a lifetime. They are pressing and difficult, often becoming wounds in the soul of the person who yearns for the power and courage of hope, especially in stressful times.

The Vintage Spiritual Classics present the testimony of writers across the centuries who have considered all these difficulties and who have pondered the mysterious ways, unfathomable mercies, and deep consolations afforded by God to those who call upon Him from out of the depths of their lives. These writers, then, are our companions, even our champions, in a common effort to discern the meaning of God in personal experience. For God is personal to us. To whom does He speak if not to us, provided we have the desire to hear Him deep within our hearts?

Each volume opens with a specially commissioned essay by a well-known contemporary writer that offers the reader an appreciation of its intrinsic value. A chronology of the general historical context of each author and his work is provided, as are suggestions for further reading.

We offer a final word about the act of reading these spiritual classics. From the very earliest accounts of monastic practice—dating back to the fourth century—it is evident that a form of reading called *lectio divina* ("divine" or "spiritual reading") was essential to any deliberate spiritual life. This kind of reading is quite different from that of scanning a text for useful facts and bits of information, or advancing along an exciting plot line to a climax in the action. It is, rather, a meditative approach by which the reader seeks to savor and taste the beauty and truth of every phrase and passage. This process of contemplative reading has the effect of enkindling in the reader compunction for past behavior that has been less than beautiful and true. At the same time, it increases the desire to seek a realm where all that is lovely and unspoiled may be found. There are four steps in *lectio divina:* first to read, next to meditate, then to rest in the sense of God's nearness, and, ultimately, to resolve to govern one's actions in the light of new understanding. This kind of reading is itself an act of prayer. And, indeed, it is in prayer that God manifests His Presence to us.

by Avery Dulles, S.J.

The Spiritual Exercises of St. Ignatius of Loyola ranks high among the classics of Christian spirituality. According to a plausible estimate in 1948, the book had by then been published some 4,500 times; and about four and a half million copies had been printed.[1] These figures would have to be greatly increased to cover the next fifty years. *The Spiritual Exercises* is, of course, the basic text for Jesuit spirituality, but many other religious orders have adopted the text. *The Exercises,* given in a variety of forms, have been used in countless numbers of retreats for priests, religious, and laypersons all over the world and are as much in use today as ever in the past.

At first sight, *The Spiritual Exercises* is unprepossessing. Hardly a book at all, it is little more than a set of notes for directors of retreats. Made up of sections composed at different times and for different purposes, it resists continuous reading. For all that, it recapitulates some of the finest fruits of medieval spirituality and stands at the opening of a new age. It thus marks a crucial turning point in the history of Catholic spirituality.

St. Ignatius, as much as any individual, might be said to represent the transition from medieval to modern Catholicism. He and his companions, even before they became aware of the Reformation as a threat, were at work revitalizing the faith in southern Europe. In the mid-sixteenth century they vigorously opposed the tide of the Reformation in regions such as Austria, Bavaria, the Rhineland, and Poland. They struggled mightily to recapture En-

gland and Scotland for the Catholic faith. They spearheaded the
Church's missionary thrust to the New World of the Americas as
well as to Northern Africa, India, and East Asia. Favoring the
growing centralization of the Church, they worked closely with
the popes, as have their successors even to our own generation. In
all these endeavors they used *The Spiritual Exercises* as their handbook.

The book was substantially complete before Ignatius became a
priest and the principal founder of the Society of Jesus. Except
obliquely in several of the "Rules for Thinking with the Church"
(sections 352–370), the book contains no reference to the Reformation. Its origin must be traced to the conversion of Ignatius himself
from his first career as a dapper young Spanish courtier to his second career as a companion of Jesus.

In 1521 Iñigo de Loyola (as he was then called) was a gentleman
in the service of the viceroy of Navarre. In that capacity he was
summoned to assist in the defense of a section of Navarre claimed
by the French with the backing of King Francis I. Stubbornly
resisting the assault against Pamplona in the face of hopeless odds,
Ignatius was struck by enemy fire, which shattered his right leg.
The French soldiers, impressed by his valor and nobility of character, gave him preliminary medical attention and then released him
to be carried on a stretcher by his fellow countrymen to his home
castle at Loyola, where he spent the next year painfully recovering.

During his recuperation he asked for reading material, prefer-
ably romances of chivalry such as *Amadis of Gaul*. But the castle
could offer him only two books. The first was a four-volume Spanish translation of the *Life of Christ* by the Carthusian Ludolph of
Saxony (d. 1377); the other was the *Golden Legend* by the Dominican Jacopo of Varazze (d. 1298)—a collection of lives of the saints
arranged according to the order of their feasts throughout the
Church year. As Ignatius lay in bed, his thoughts alternated
between the prospect of worldly glory and the following of Christ.
When he thought of his future life in terms of serving an exalted
lady at court and performing great feats of arms, he was initially
delighted, as he also was when he contemplated the exploits of St.
Francis and St. Dominic as models to be followed. But there was a
difference. The secular romances left a certain dryness and restless-

ness in their wake, whereas the sacred scenarios left him peaceful and contented even after his attention turned to other things.

Ignatius was at that time making what he would later call an "election." He was in the throes of deciding what to do with his life. Would he return to court and aspire to worldly glory, or would he dedicate himself to the following of Christ in meekness and poverty? For making this decision, a "discernment of spirits" was required. By introspection he found that he was being tossed about by a spirit of holiness and a spirit of worldliness. The "Election" (in this translation called "Choice of a Way of Life")² and the "Discernment of Spirits" constitute the very core of *The Spiritual Exercises,* which Ignatius composed by bits and pieces over the next twenty years.

The essentials were produced in the first few years, especially in 1522–23. Leaving the castle of Loyola in February 1522, Ignatius traveled by mule across the northern tier of Spain to the Marian shrine at Montserrat, located at an abbey high above Barcelona. After an all-night vigil before the altar of the Virgin Mary at the Abbey of Montserrat, he made a general confession to a monk of that community, covering the sins of his entire life. He then exchanged his rich garments with the rags of a beggar and settled at the nearby town of Manresa, with the intention of writing down some spiritual reflections before going to the seaport of Barcelona. Delaying his departure, he remained at Manresa for eleven months as a solitary hermit in a cave, living by handouts as a beggar and making the very exercises he was to describe in the book. He paid occasional visits to Montserrat, where his confessor seems to have loaned him the book of *Exercises for the Spiritual Life* by the former abbot of Montserrat, García de Cisneros. He also borrowed a copy of the *Imitation of Christ,* which was then ascribed to the Frenchman Jean de Gerson (d. 1428) but is now ascribed to the German Thomas à Kempis (d. 1471). So devoted was Ignatius to this spiritual classic that he read a chapter a day for the rest of his life and had it on a table at his bedside when he died.

In March 1523 Ignatius embarked from Barcelona to make a pilgrimage to the Holy Land, hoping to labor for the good of souls in places sanctified by the presence of the Savior. When forbidden to remain in Jerusalem because of the tense relations between Chris-

tians and Moslems, he returned to Spain. Recognizing the importance of learning for an effective apostolate, he began to study
Latin at Barcelona (1524–25) and then applied himself to philosophy and theology at Alcalá (1526) and Salamanca (1527). During
his studies he engaged in spiritual conversations with men and
women, seeking to win them to a better way of life and to enrich
their life of prayer. We may suppose that many of the rules and
instructions in *The Exercises,* such as the Three Methods of Prayer,
the methods of Daily and General Examinations of Conscience,
and the Rules with Regard to Eating, for the Distribution of Alms,
and for Scruples represent the kind of advice he was dispensing at
that stage of his career.

Ignatius's studies in Spain went poorly, partly because he took
courses for which he was insufficiently prepared and partly because
he was distracted by his activities of preaching and spiritual direction. He was also denounced several times to the Inquisition, and
even imprisoned, on the suspicion that he might be one of the trou-
blesome "illuminati" *(alumbrados)* who were advocating direct
guidance by the Holy Spirit without recourse to the mediation of
the Church.

For all these reasons, Ignatius decided to transfer his activities to
the University of Paris, where he devoted himself more systemati-
cally to studies for seven more years (1528–35). While at Paris he
gathered a remarkable group of half a dozen fellow students, and
all of them took vows of poverty and chastity together at Montmartre on the Feast of the Assumption, August 15, 1534. Although
these men were not yet Jesuits, they were laying the foundations of
the future Society of Jesus.

The members of this little band had all made *The Spiritual Exercises* under Ignatius and had their lives revolutionized by the experience. Most of them soon began to give the Exercises to others, but
in order for them to do so, a text was required for their guidance.
The earliest surviving versions of the book, in the form of notes
taken by retreatants, date from this Paris period. Later in Rome,
about 1539 or 1540, Ignatius made a few revisions and additions.
The "autograph" text, dating from about 1545, is a Spanish text
with corrections in the handwriting of Ignatius and is the principal
source for most modern editions, including the present one. The

first translation into Latin (the *versio prima*), which exists in several manuscript editions, was probably the work of Ignatius himself. The first printed edition was an elegant Latin translation by André des Freux (the *versio vulgata*). It was published anonymously in 1548 together with a papal bull of approbation.

The Spiritual Exercises may be described as a handbook for retreat directors, not as a book to be read by retreatants. It consists essentially of a series of points for meditation or contemplation, accompanied by a multitude of "Introductory Observations," "Additional Directions," "Rules," and "Notes." The overall purpose of the book is to enable exercitants to overcome their disordered inclinations, to be inflamed with the love of God, and to make firm and concrete resolutions about how to follow Christ more closely.

The retreatant is supposed to take about a month to go through the entire course of *The Exercises,* spending four or five hours each day in intense prayer. The material is distributed in four "weeks," the approximate period normally given to each of the four segments. Each "week" has its own distinct objective.

Week I is a period of conversion from a life of sin to one of observance of God's commandments, corresponding to what was classically known as the "purgative" way—the purification of the soul required for it to turn away from evil and advance toward God. The predominant themes are repentance for sin, fear of eternal punishment, and hope of God's merciful forgiveness through the crucified Christ. The spirit of this first week is encapsulated in the "colloquy" at the end of the First Exercise, in which the exercitant converses with Christ on the cross and then puts to himself the questions: "What have I done for Christ? What am I doing for Christ? What ought I to do for Christ?" (section 53).

Week II is one of progress from mere observance of the commandments to a life of generous service, prompted by the love of Christ and the desire to follow him more closely. It corresponds to what in classical spirituality was known as the "illuminative" way—the acquisition of virtues in imitation of Christ. This week is especially designed for those who wish "to give greater proof of their love, and to distinguish themselves in the service of the eternal King" (section 97). They are to be moved by a desire to imitate

Christ, who embraced poverty and endured insults and injuries out of love for us.

Week III is a time of mystical identification with Christ's suffering, marked by the desire to weep and grieve with him. Week IV, which concludes *The Exercises*, is a period of joyful communion with the risen Christ. These two last weeks together correspond to the "unitive" or "perfective" way of traditional mysticism, a phase characterized by intimate and habitual union with God. The expectation is that the resolutions made in Week II will be confirmed by these further meditations.

The entire course of *The Exercises* is framed by the "First Principle and Foundation" at the beginning and the "Contemplation to Obtain Divine Love" at the end. Week II is introduced by a contemplation on "The Kingdom of Christ," which prepares the way for several other key exercises connected with the "Choice of a Way of Life"—namely, the "Two Standards," the "Three Classes of Men," and the "Three Kinds of Humility."

Reflecting as it does the conversion of Ignatius, *The Spiritual Exercises* has been the instrument of countless conversions. Through the structured sequence of exercises, it can lead to the renunciation of sin and, beyond this, to joyful and committed discipleship. While avoiding any undue coercion, Ignatius draws the exercitant forward by logical steps to ever greater degrees of generosity in the following of Christ. He puts the retreatant in direct communication with Jesus, who speaks through the Gospels. The colloquies at the end of the meditations on the "Kingdom of Christ" and on the "Two Standards" quintessentially express the Ignatian ideal of reverent service.

Ideally, *The Exercises* are to be presented to a single exercitant, who spends a month in solitude, without interruption by any business or social contacts. The exercitant meets several times a day with the director, who speaks with the person about what he or she is experiencing and recommends suitable subjects for the meditations of that day. But even in the time of Ignatius, *The Exercises* were sometimes administered to groups. They were given to laymen and laywomen as well as to clerics and religious.

With his characteristic realism, Ignatius provided for situations other than the ideal. As can be seen from the text, he knows that many retreatants, lacking the required ability or suitable dispositions, are not prepared for the full *Exercises*. The director, he says, should take account of the age, health, education, attitudes, and circumstances of each exercitant.

For those who are beginners in the spiritual life, Ignatius recommends giving only the material pertaining to the First Week. Such persons can be dismissed after being taught how to examine their consciences and confess their sins, and after resolving to go forward in the way of the commandments (section 18).

Others, who have the capacity and disposition to make the full course of *Exercises,* may not be able to disengage themselves from their day-to-day responsibilities. Without going into seclusion, they may stretch out the meditations over a longer period of time, praying for about an hour and a half each day (section 19).

In all cases the director is to use great prudence in deciding whether the exercitant is ready to pass on to the next meditation, the next day, or the next week. For proper adaptation, it is essential that the retreatant frankly manifest his or her thoughts, temptations, and sentiments to the director.

The extraordinary success of the book is certainly not due to its literary qualities. Ignatius writes in a very concise style. He avoids literary flourishes, perhaps because they would be an obstacle rather than an aid to his objectives. The order of presentation could seem confusing. The succession of meditations is interrupted by sets of rules and notes that might irritate the casual reader. But these rules are for the director who gives *The Exercises*; they are not written for the retreatants themselves. Anyone reading the text should keep these facts in mind.

Judged by its own standards, the book is well written. Every expression is chosen with great deliberation to convey exactly what the author has in mind. Using words in an original way, Ignatius in this text established a vocabulary that has endured throughout five centuries of Christian spirituality.

Ignatius was in many respects conservative. His spirituality was nourished, as noted, by such authors as Ludolph of Saxony, Jacopo of Varazze, and Thomas à Kempis. His theology is quite traditional and resistant to the biblical criticism of humanists such as

Desiderius Erasmus (d. 1536) and to the doctrinal innovations of the Reformers. His social and political ideas reflect the order of Christian feudalism. Much of his imagery is derived from life at court, from military life, and from the Crusades. He looks upon God as "his sovereign Majesty" and compares God to an earthly king. Ignatius has occasionally been likened to Don Quixote, who was incongruously wedded to the mentality of a dying age.

But from another point of view, Ignatius stands on the cusp of modernity. Unlike his medieval predecessors, he is not content to accept the existing state of things as a given. He sees it rather as a challenge and an opportunity for creative responses. Touched by the humanism of the Renaissance, Ignatius puts the human being at center stage. *Homo*—"man" in the present translation—is the first word of the inaugural exercise (section 23). This man is seen as being responsible for his own fate. He can either cooperate with grace or refuse it; he can save or lose his soul. With his expansive vision of the whole world to be conquered for Christ, Ignatius is a spiritual counterpart of the Spanish conquistador. He exemplifies a characteristically Renaissance optimism about the possibilities of human enterprise.

Ignatius is modern, also, in his respect for the individuality and freedom of each person. He tells the director to let the exercitant deal directly with God and thus to be, in the expression of Carl Rogers, "nondirective." All the powers of the individual are to be engaged—the intellect, the memory, the imagination, the heart, the will, and the senses. In making the meditations, the individual is to decide what he or she desires, and to stay with a given point so long as it satisfies the soul, without feeling any obligation to cover all the material proposed. In contemplating the mysteries of the life of Christ, the retreatant is asked to compose the scene—to decide whether the road from Nazareth to Bethlehem is broad or narrow, level or steep, and so forth (section 112; cf. 192). The exercitant will also decide on the basis of personal experience what posture to adopt in prayer: whether to walk or be still, whether to stand, kneel, sit, or lie prostrate (sections 76, 239).

Modern, too, is Ignatius's appreciation for creativity. The written text is open-ended and is to be completed, in the first place, by the director and, secondly, by the exercitant, who responds to the

questions raised by meditation on the texts. Even the exercitant is
not finally in charge. Since the real objective is to perceive the will
of God, God has the last word.[3] In making choices, we have to
implore God for "the grace not to be deaf to his call, but prompt
and diligent to accomplish his holy will" (section 91). Notwith-
standing his emphasis on human freedom, Ignatius avoids the trap
of Pelagian self-sufficiency.[4]

In his appreciation for the direct communion between the soul
and God, Ignatius discloses the mystical side of his temperament.
One can understand why he was under suspicion of being an illu-
minist. But this tendency is balanced by its polar opposite. Ignatius
is emphatically a man of the Church. He is perfectly clear that we
are never permitted to do what the Church prohibits (section 170).
In his "Rules for Thinking with the Church" he sharply diverges
from the Protestant Reformers and even, it would seem, from
some Catholic reformers, such as Erasmus. As a good soldier in the
army of Christ, Ignatius submits his judgment totally to that of the
hierarchy and expects others to do the same (section 353). A key
feature of Ignatian asceticism is the mortification of one's own will
by unquestioning obedience to religious superiors. Such obedience
is to be shown especially to the pope, whom Ignatius venerates as
the "vicar of Christ on earth."[5]

Although written for retreatants, *The Spiritual Exercises* is much
more than a manual for retreats. It is the distillation of the spiritual
wisdom of one of the great masters of the practical life. The book
can be used, for example, as a school of prayer. With the utmost
conciseness, Ignatius sets forth a great variety of methods. Within
the text of *The Exercises,* we find considerations, meditations, contemplations, and applications of the senses. And in the "Three
Methods of Prayer," he speaks of various forms of vocal prayer
(sections 238–260). He shows a particular predilection for three
vocal prayers, all used in the triple colloquies (sections 63, 147): the
"Our Father," the "Soul of Christ," and the "Hail Mary."[6]

In or outside retreats, many people use the principles given by
St. Ignatius for arriving at decisions of fundamental importance for
their lives. The directives for "Making a Choice for a Way of Life"
(sections 169–188) and for "Amendment and Reformation of One's
Way of Living" (section 189), together with the two sets of "Rules

for the Discernment of Spirits" (sections 313–344), have been enor-
mously influential. Ignatius proposed an original way of using
one's affections as a guide to decision making, always in the context
of meditations on the Gospels.

For those who wish to ponder the wisdom of Ignatius outside
the framework of a retreat, the text offers any number of profound
principles. For example, the concept of "indifference" in the First
Principle and Foundation (section 23; cf. 179); the rule of using created things in the measure that they help us achieve the goal of life
(section 23); the ideal of wishing to express one's love of Christ by
sharing in his sufferings and his joys (sections 48, 195, 197, 206, 221,
229); the importance of "acting against" unruly inclinations and
doing the opposite of what we are tempted to do (sections 13, 16, 97,
325, 350, 351); the techniques for controlling one's desires and
affections by the use of external circumstances and the imagination
(sections 74, 78–81, 206, 229); the idea that love "ought to manifest
itself in deeds rather than in words" (section 230). These and
dozens of other maxims, taken from *The Exercises,* have assisted
generations of faithful Christians to go forward in the footsteps of
Christ.

Educators in the Jesuit tradition have modeled their pedagogy
on *The Exercises.* They have remembered that students derive
"greater spiritual fruit and relish" from what they discover for
themselves, rather than being told everything by their teachers
(section 2). The teacher should avoid proposing matter that is "too
subtle and advanced" for the student to understand (section 9).
Educators, moreover, should be conscious that "it is not much
knowledge that fills and satisfies the soul, but the intimate understanding and relish of the truth" (section 2).

The Spiritual Exercises, as I have already indicated, is a book of its
own time. The exegesis is untouched by modern historical-critical
approaches to Scripture. Like his contemporaries, Ignatius believed
that good and evil spirits continually intervene in the world of
experience. He wrote against the background of a Christendom
ruled by monarchs and disposed to wage war against the infidel.
All of these points challenge the retreat director of our day to be
creative, adapting *The Exercises* to the mentality of later genera-

tions. As we have noted, Ignatius insisted on the need to adapt them to various audiences in different times and places.

Although *The Spiritual Exercises* was not written primarily for Jesuits, Jesuits have consistently used the book as a source for their spirituality. The meditations on "The Kingdom of Christ" and "The Two Standards" have taught them to think of themselves as called to be soldiers in an army dedicated to conquer souls for Christ under the banner of the cross. For Jesuits and others *The Exercises* have elicited and sustained the courage, discipline, self-denial, and perseverance needed to do great things for Christ.

Although St. Ignatius made no pretense of being an original speculative theologian, his *Spiritual Exercises* have had a significant impact on theology. The Ignatian accent on freedom was particularly influential. In the sixteenth-century debates about free will and grace, Jesuit theologians consistently defended human freedom against any who might seem to compromise that freedom for the sake of safeguarding the divine sovereignty. In the ensuing centuries many Jesuits wrote in opposition to absolutist monarchies and in favor of the free society. It is no mere coincidence, then, that the chief architect of Vatican II's Declaration on Religious Freedom was an American Jesuit, John Courtney Murray.

Pursuing other themes in *The Exercises,* Jesuits in the nineteenth century contributed to the revival of Thomism and the reinforcement of papal primacy. Within recent memory Jesuit theologians such as Karl Rahner, Henri de Lubac, Teilhard de Chardin, and Bernard Lonergan confessed their immense indebtedness to *The Exercises,* as did the erstwhile Jesuit Hans Urs von Balthasar.[7] The principles of St. Ignatius will presumably continue to generate new insights as theologians reflect on the human condition and human destiny in the light of faith. As a classic text, *The Spiritual Exercises* has inexhaustible fecundity.

Early Life

1491—Ignatius, seventh and youngest son of Beltrán Ibañez de Oñaz y Loyola and Marina Sanchez de Licona, is born in Azpeitia in the Basque province of Guipúzcoa in northern Spain. Basque society is thoroughly Catholic, though feuding and illicit marital unions are common. His pious mother has Ignatius tonsured at an early age. This signifies that he is dedicated to the clerical state.

1492—Christopher Columbus sails to the New World.

Pope Innocent VIII dies, and Roderigo Borgia becomes Pope Alexander VI.

1493—Frederick III dies and is succeeded as Holy Roman Emperor by Maximilian I.

The Turks invade Dalmatia and Croatia. Charles VIII of France prepares to invade Italy.

1494—The Wars of Italy commence when Charles VIII invades Florence and then Rome, forcing the pope to flee to Castel Sant' Angelo.

1495—Charles VIII is crowned king of Naples, which he claims as his hereditary right. Ferdinand II of Spain reconquers Naples. French soldiers contract syphilis in Italy and cause an epidemic to spread throughout Europe.

1497—Savonarola is excommunicated for attempting to depose Pope Alexander VI.

1498—Vasco da Gama rounds the Cape of Good Hope and discovers the maritime route to the Indies.

Charles VIII of France dies and Louis XII becomes king.

Erasmus of Rotterdam teaches at Oxford. Savonarola is burned at the stake in Florence.

1499—Amerigo Vespucci and Alonso de Ojeda sail from Spain on an exploratory voyage to South America.

1503—Giuliano della Rovere becomes pope, taking the name of Julius II at the death of Pope Alexander VI.

1504—Queen Isabella of Spain dies at age fifty-three, leaving King Ferdinand to lead Spain forward against French aggression in Italy, their common battleground.

Under the Treaty of Lyons, Louis XII cedes Naples to Ferdinand II, establishing Naples under Spanish control.

Maximilian I begins the transformation of the Holy Roman Empire into a universal Hapsburg monarchy.

1506—At age fifteen Ignatius is sent four hundred miles from his birthplace to his father's friend, Juan Velázquez de Cuéllar, chief treasurer of King Ferdinand, to be educated as a Castilian gentleman. There Ignatius learns to ride, fence, dance, and sing. He reads novels of chivalry, the popular literature of the Spanish Renaissance. Though he has received tonsure, Ignatius dresses fashionably in bright colors and a flowing cape with a feather in his cap and sword and dagger at his waist. He leads a worldly life centered on pleasure, ambition, and vainglory. He is passionate about gambling, flirtatious with women, and quick with his sword.

1509—Henry VIII becomes king of England and marries Catherine of Aragon.

France declares war on Venice, and is victorious.

1511—Pope Julius II establishes the Holy League with Venice and Aragon to force the French out of Italy.

1512—The French defeat Spain at Ravenna.

1513—Leo X becomes pope on the death of Julius II.

1514—European ships reach the waters of China.

1515—Scandal in Azpeitia. On one of his periodic visits home to the castle of Loyola, Ignatius and several friends enter into a dispute with Anchieta, the former rector of the church of San Sebastián de Soreasu, of which the Loyola family is patron. The disagreement revolves around who has the right to name the new rector, since Anchieta has retired from the position. Charges are brought against Ignatius for instigating some form of violence against the parish clergy on Shrove Tuesday, February 20. The charges are eventually dropped, but Ignatius ever after bears remorse for the scandal he has caused.

Francis I becomes king of France. He conquers Milan.

1516—King Ferdinand II of Spain dies. The future emperor Charles V becomes King Charles I of Spain. Juan Velázquez de Cuéllar is dismissed from his post and dies in 1517. Ignatius returns home to the Basque country.

Erasmus publishes an edition of the New Testament in Greek and Latin. Sir Thomas More publishes *Utopia*.

1517—Ignatius enters the service of Don Antonio Manrique de Lara, Duke of Nájera, who has recently become viceroy of Navarre, a region of the Pyrenees straddling Spain and France.

Luther publishes his Ninety-Five Theses at Wittenberg, questioning the legitimacy of the sale of indulgences by the Church and challenging the authority of the pope. This traditionally marks the beginning of the Reformation in Germany.

1518—Cardinal Wolsey crafts the Peace of London between Spain, England, France, the pope, and Emperor Maximilian I.

1519—Charles I of Spain becomes Holy Roman Emperor as Charles V on the death of Maximilian I.

Hernando Cortés arrives in Mexico and is received by Montezuma, the Aztec king. He brings with him Arabian horses. He will take chocolate back to Spain.

Ferdinand Magellan leaves Europe under Spanish sponsorship to circumnavigate the globe.

Former Catholic priest Ulrich Zwingli preaches in Geneva against indulgences and church ceremonies. He proposes radical reforms, claiming Scripture as the sole guide to belief. The Swiss Reformation begins.

1520—Suleiman I, the Magnificent, becomes Sultan of Turkey.

The Anabaptist movement begins in Germany under Thomas Münzer, who taught an extreme form of Reformation stressing adult baptism as an outward profession of faith. He emphasized the rule of faith as purely the inspiration of the Holy Spirit needing no external authority, not even Scripture.

Pope Leo X excommunicates Luther with the bull *Exsurge Domine,* which Luther then publicly burns. The Church declares him both heretic and outlaw.

Conversion

1521—Cortes gains control of Mexico by destroying the Aztec state.

Sultan Suleiman I defeats Belgrade and invades Hungary.

Pope Leo X names Henry VIII "Defender of the Faith" for defending the seven sacraments against Luther. Luther is banned from the Holy Roman Empire. He begins translating the Bible into German while secluded in Wartburg Castle.

French troops attack the city of Pamplona on May 17. In his own words, speaking of himself in the third person, Ignatius describes his participation in the fight:

> He was in a fortress besieged by the French. All his companions-in-arms were of the opinion that they should surrender if their lives were spared, for they saw clearly that defense was impossible. But he urged so many contrary arguments on the commandant that he persuaded him to go on resisting, in spite of the unanimous view of the other *caballeros*. Indeed, they took heart at witnessing his courage and exertions. On the day when they expected to be bombarded, he confessed his sins to one of his companions-in-arms. The attack had gone on for some considerable time when a cannonball struck one of his legs and shattered it completely, at the same time passing between his legs, wounding the other gravely. At his fall, the others in the fortress immediately surrendered to the French, who on entering treated the wounded man very handsomely, being courteous and friendly. After lying twelve or fifteen days in Pamplona, he was carried on a litter to his own country, where he became extremely ill. Doctors and surgeons were called in from many places, and decided that the leg must be dislocated again, as the bones were out of position either through faulty work (by the French surgeons) or because they had become disarranged on the journey. As it was, the leg could not heal. So they began

xxx CHRONOLOGY

anew that butchery, during which, as in all those he had suffered so far and was still to suffer, he never spoke a word nor
showed any sign of pain, except by tightly clenching his fists.
In spite of everything his condition worsened. He lost the
power of taking nourishment, and the other symptoms which
herald the approach of death appeared. By the feast of the
Nativity of St. John the Baptist (June 24), the doctors had very
little hope of saving him, and he was counselled to make his
confession, so he received the sacraments on the eve of SS.
Peter and Paul (June 29). The doctors said that if he did not
show a turn for the better before midnight, he might be
counted for dead. Now, the sick man always had a devotion to
St. Peter, so it pleased our Lord that he should begin to feel
better precisely at midnight, and his recovery was so rapid
that after a few days he was pronounced to be out of danger.
(from James Brodrick, S.J., *Saint Ignatius Loyola: The Pilgrim
Years, 1491–1538* [San Francisco: Ignatius Press, 1998], pp. 57–
58)

Ignatius is carried home to Casa Loyola, where he is cared for by his
brother's wife, Magdalena. He endures further agonizing surgery
as one bone had become superimposed on another in his right
knee, making that leg unsightly and shorter than the left. He is
immobilized for some time, and during his long convalescence, to
pass the time, he asks for books of romance and chivalry. But the
only books to be found in the house are *The Life of Christ* by the
German Carthusian Ludolph of Saxony and the popular collection
of the lives of the saints, *The Golden Legend,* both in Castilian. His
heart is inflamed by reading about the heroic dedication of the saints.

Ignatius asks himself if he can follow Christ as did the great saints
Augustine, Francis of Assisi, and Dominic. He is prompted by
their example to review his past conduct. He determines to do
penance for his sins and, from this moment, to imitate the saints
with all the generosity of his being. A clear vision one night of our
Lady with the Holy Child Jesus confirms him in his desire to break
with his past life. Ignatius vows never again to indulge in or consent to carnal desire.

1522—Adrian VI becomes pope at the death of Leo X.

By late winter Ignatius's leg has healed, and he sets out on a pilgrimage to Jerusalem. He travels to make an all-night vigil at the altar of Our Lady of Montserrat near Barcelona. He gives away his fine clothes to a beggar and puts on the sackcloth garment he desires to wear as a pilgrim. He then leaves for Barcelona but detours to stop at nearby Manresa for a rest before sailing on to Italy and thence to the Holy Land.

Ignatius remains in Manresa for ten months, fasting, praying for hours every day, fighting his excessive scrupulosity about sin, and giving spiritual advice to others. During this time he reads *The Imitation of Christ* by Thomas à Kempis, which he carries with him ever after for daily meditation. God grants him the grace of many illuminations at this time from which he gains profound mystical knowledge of the Trinity, God's act of Creation, the presence of Christ in the Eucharist, and the humanity of Christ and Mary. He begins to make the first notes that will eventually form *The Spiritual Exercises*.

1523—Clement VII becomes pope at the death of Adrian VI.

Ignatius leaves Barcelona to begin his pilgrimage to Jerusalem, where he arrives in September. He visits with great devotion and attention the sacred scenes of Christ's life. His incorporation of "composition of place" into the spiritual methodology of *The Exercises* receives its early formulation as a result.

Student Years

1524—The French are driven out of Italy.

Ignatius returns to Barcelona in March determined to acquire an academic foundation of learning in order to become a better spiritual teacher. During his two years of study here, he begs for his daily bread and gives Christian instruction to children and adults.

1525—Francis I is taken prisoner at Pavia, and Charles V rules Italy.

1526—In March, with a notebook containing the major part of *The Exercises* now written down, Ignatius journeys over five hundred miles barefoot from Barcelona to the University of Alcalá, near Madrid. University professors are now on intimate terms with the teachings of Erasmus and Luther. Moreover, the heresy of Illuminism, a derivative of ancient Gnosticism, is inspiring many reactionaries in the Church who have become anarchists in faith and morals. Consequently, he (Ignatius) receives the intense scrutiny of the Inquisition. For his zealous piety, and because he is lacking any clerical or academic credentials, Ignatius himself comes under suspicion. He spends forty-two days in prison. A lengthy court proceeding finally clears him of heresy, but he is forbidden to teach religion under any circumstances until he completes his studies and has a clear ecclesiastical mandate.

1527—The Sack of Rome. Art treasures are looted, 4,000 people are killed, and Pope Clement VII is confined in Castel Sant' Angelo.

With a few companions, Ignatius leaves Alcalá for Salamanca. Using what would become known as "The First Method of Prayer" in *The Exercises,* Ignatius teaches the many people who are attracted to him how to find peace of soul. He leads them through an examination of conscience based on the Ten Commandments. They then make an act of contrition and of gratitude for forgiveness, followed by a fervent Our Father. The exercise ends with a few moments of conversation with God to ask for help to do better in the future. Ignatius again comes under the suspicion of Church authorities, is briefly imprisoned, then examined and released with restrictions on his capacity to teach. Ignatius decides to leave for Paris to continue his studies, finding it impossible to obey the injunction against catechizing.

1528—Ignatius arrives in Paris in the heart of winter, having walked there barefoot behind a small donkey for more than a month, limping along mile after mile. He remains in Paris for seven years. During his impoverished years as a student, Ignatius journeys several times to Flanders, Rouen, and London to ask for support from rich Spanish merchants for himself and other poor students.

1529—Having received his bachelor's degree in Latin studies from the Collège de Montaigu at the University of Paris, Ignatius begins to prepare for his Master of Arts in philosophy at the Collège de Sainte-Barbe. Here he meets two men who become his great life-long companions in religion: Francis Xavier and Pierre Favre. Ignatius directs them in *The Spiritual Exercises* as he already has a number of other university people, some of whom even occupy teaching posts. Favre will become the first priest of the Company of Jesus. Francis Xavier will credit Ignatius with saving him from coming under the influence of anti-Roman Catholic followers of Luther, Melanchthon, Hutten, and Zwingli.

It is at this time that *The Exercises* takes on the formula of a retreat. Such a retreat called for a complete withdrawal from the world for a month of solitude during which one follows a methodical routine of prayer and meditation. Spiritual reflection is directed toward one end: to obtain, away from worldly distractions, an integration of the self in order to discover how to enter into a wholehearted dedication to God under the standard of Christ.

1530—Francis I marries Eleanor y Portugal, the sister of Charles V.

Melanchthon's *Confession of Augsburg,* one of the key documents of Lutheranism, is ratified by the Protestant princes, who ally themselves against Catholic Emperor Charles V.

1531—Henry VIII of England breaks with Rome over the question of the annulment of his first marriage to Catherine of Aragon and declares himself Supreme Head of the Church in England.

1532—John Calvin, leader of Reformed Protestantism in France, takes up studies at the new Collège de France founded in Paris by Francis I for the study of Latin, Greek, and Hebrew.

1533—Henry VIII marries Anne Boleyn and is excommunicated by the pope.

On March 15 Ignatius receives his Licentiate degree, which allows him to teach in Paris or anywhere else in the world. He now leads a group of six men who call themselves "friends in the Lord" and who are committed to serve Christ. Ignatius, no less aware than Luther of the abuses of clerical authority in the Church, adds an appendix to *The Exercises* that lays down rules for acting in a spirit of holiness in the work of the Church. Above all, he urges obedience, devotion, and loyalty to "Holy Mother Church."

Anti-Catholic propaganda is widely circulated in French towns. Many statues of the Virgin Mary are mutilated.

The Company of Jesus

1534—Francis I is enraged when posters denouncing the Roman Mass are posted all over Paris and other cities. He succeeds in arresting over two hundred Lutherans and burning twenty-five at the stake.

Pope Clement VII dies. Cardinal Alessandro Farnese becomes Pope Paul III. The new pope rebukes King Francis.

In Paris, Ignatius marches in the processions of the Blessed Sacrament, which are held to make repentance for the cruelty meted out to the Lutherans.

Ignatius finally scrapes together the necessary money for fees and receives his diploma of Master of Arts on March 14. He then enters a course of theological studies at the Dominican convent of Saint-Jacques and at a nearby Franciscan convent. He studies Peter Lombard's *Sentences* and the works of Thomas Aquinas, both of which enrich his own spirituality immensely.

On August 15, the feast of the Assumption of Our Lady, Ignatius and his six friends (including Pierre Favre and Francis Xavier) vow to live in religious community together. They promise to exercise chastity and poverty and pledge obedience to the pope. Pierre Favre, the only priest among them, says Mass for them in a small Montmartre chapel. This marks the birth of the Company of Jesus, which dedicates itself to work in Palestine for the salvation of the Turks.

1535—Sir Thomas More refuses to take the oath of supremacy to Henry VIII and is executed.

Francis I issues an edict for the extirpation of the Lutheran sect in France.

Ignatius falls ill and suffers immensely from a recurring stomach ailment. Vomiting, fever, heavy sweats, and agonizing pain afflict him for hours at a time. He has chronic cystitis associated with gallstones. On his doctors' advice, he returns home to Guipúzcoa to recuperate.

1536—Anne Boleyn is executed in the Tower of London. Henry VIII marries Jane Seymour. The English Parliament declares papal authority void in England.

John Calvin publishes the *Institutes of the Christian Religion,* a defense of French Protestant beliefs.

Ignatius travels from Spain to Venice to continue his studies of theology and to give *The Exercises* to a number of eminent persons in that city. He awaits the arrival of his companions, who must make a perilous journey from Paris across Europe, the scene of ongoing conflict between Charles V and Francis I.

Rome

1537—Jane Seymour, Queen of England, dies after the birth of Prince Edward.

Ignatius's companions arrive in Venice in January. Their intention is to make a pilgrimage together to Palestine. But war with Turkey appears imminent, and no ships are sailing. They then prepare themselves for Holy Orders. Ignatius and five companions are ordained on June 24. Ignatius travels to Vicenza for a year to make spiritual preparation for his first Mass while the others go on to Rome. He experiences profound spiritual consolations. On his way to Rome, he has a mystical vision at La Storta, a small village on the Via Cassia, in which he perceives himself to be chosen by Christ to lead a society dedicated totally to Him. For this final long journey of his life, he walks more than 350 miles on his game leg.

1538—Ignatius says his first Mass on Christmas Day in a chapel adjoining the basilica of Saint Mary Major. He weeps for joy so copiously that it takes him more than an hour to finish since he can scarcely read the missal through his tears.

While living in Rome, Ignatius and his companions engage in many charitable enterprises in addition to catechizing. These include opening a shelter for the indigent during the harsh winter and feeding over three thousand people.

While preaching at this time against Lutheran heresies, Ignatius is persecuted by Agostino Mainardi, an Augustinian friar who is sympathetic to Lutheran teaching and who would himself soon leave the Church. Slanderous lies are spread about Ignatius, and people are afraid to listen to his sermons. Ignatius seeks out Pope Paul III and explains everything in full to him. A final sentence from the pope exonerates Ignatius. Since Palestine is out of reach, Ignatius and his companions offer their services to the pope and promise to accept whatever work he asks them to do for the good of the Church.

1539—Hernando de Soto explores Florida; Claus Magnus draws a map of the world.

Ignatius and his followers deliberate about whether they should form themselves into a new religious order, one that would be quite distinct from traditional monastic life. The new order is to be

mobile, made up of apostles of Christ who are willing to live anywhere in the world in order to serve the greater glory of God and
the good of souls. Ignatius drafts five chapters of "A First Sketch of
the Institute of the Society of Jesus." Pope Paul III gives them oral
approval.

Society of Jesus

1540—Henry VIII marries Anne of Cleves. When this marriage is
annulled, he is married for the fifth time to Catherine Howard.

Venice and Turkey sign a treaty at Constantinople.

The *Five Chapters of the Institute of the Society of Jesus* are given for-
mal approval by Pope Paul III on September 27 with the bull *Regi-
mini militantis Ecclesiae.*

Francis Xavier leaves for Portuguese India. When letters from his
master, Ignatius, arrive, he kneels down to read them.

1541—In March Ignatius begins to write the *Constitutions for the
Society of Jesus,* also known as the Jesuit Order. He is elected superior general of the Society on April 6 and finally accepts on April
19. Ignatius leads the Society until his death fifteen years later. He
and his companions make their solemn profession as members of
the Society on April 22.

1542—Pope Paul III establishes the Inquisition in Rome.

1543—Henry VIII marries for the sixth time to Catherine Parr.
She will survive him.

Pope Paul III issues the Index of Forbidden Books.

The Portuguese land in Japan.

Protestants are burned at the stake by the Spanish Inquisition.

Jesuits preach and catechize in Germany, where they also give *The Exercises*. The House of Saint Martha for women in difficulty and a house for catechumens are established in Rome.

1544—Pope Paul III calls for the Council of Trent in the papal bull *Laetare Jerusalem*. His goals are to heal the schism with the Protestants, reform the Church, and prepare a defense against the Ottoman Turks.

1545—The Council of Trent convenes.

1546—Martin Luther dies.

The first Jesuit province is created to administer the affairs of the order in Portugal. Simon Rodríguez is named provincial.

1547—Henry VIII dies and is succeeded by Edward VI.

Francis I dies and is succeeded by Henry II.

Antonio Araoz is named the first Jesuit provincial of Spain.

1548—*The Spiritual Exercises* are approved by Pope Paul III and are published.

Francis Xavier arrives in Japan and founds a mission.

1549—Pope Paul III dies.

A new Jesuit province is established in India with Francis Xavier as provincial.

1550—Cardinal Giovanni Maria del Monte becomes Pope Julius III.

1551—The Jesuits officially found the Roman College as a papal university.

Due to ill health, Ignatius submits his resignation as superior general, but it is not accepted.

1552—Pope Julius III authorizes the Society to confer university degrees.

On December 3, Francis Xavier dies, off the coast of China.

Ignatius finishes writing the *Constitutions of the Society of Jesus.*

A papal bull establishes the German College of the Society in Rome.

1553—Mary I, daughter of Henry VIII and Catherine of Aragon, becomes queen of England following the death of Edward VI.

Ignatius establishes Sicily and Brazil as new Jesuit provinces.

1554—Queen Mary I marries Philip of Spain, the son of Emperor Charles V.

Ignatius asks the Jesuit priests in Rome to choose a vicar general to assist him in governing the Society. Jerōnimo Nadal is elected.

1555—Ferdinand I and the German Electors negotiate the Peace of Augsburg, which gives Lutheran states equal civil rights with those of Roman Catholics.

Pope Julius III dies March 23. Cardinal Marcello Cervini becomes Pope Marcellus II and dies April 30. Cardinal Giovanni Pietro Caraffa becomes Pope Paul IV.

A Jesuit province is established for France.

1556—Charles V retires, abdicating his throne. His son Philip II becomes king of Spain, and his brother Ferdinand I becomes emperor of the Holy Roman Empire.

Two new Jesuit provinces are created for Lower and Upper Germany.

At 5:30 in the morning of July 31, Ignatius of Loyola dies at the end of a night of silent agony punctuated only by the cry, "My God!" He is buried on August 1 in the church of Our Lady della Strada.

1609—Ignatius is beatified on July 27 by Pope Paul V.

1622—Ignatius of Loyola and his beloved friend, Francis Xavier, are canonized saints together on March 12.

At his death, the Society of Jesus numbers 1,000 members in 76 houses in 12 provinces, including Brazil, Japan, and India. Ignatius had opened 33 colleges and 6 more had been approved. By 1645 there are 372 colleges sharing a common curriculum and a centralized government in Rome. In 1710, there are 612 with over 100 seminaries. Jesuit missionaries carried the work of Christian education to every part of the world, marching to papal authority and dedicated, in the words of their motto, "To the greater glory of God."

Today there are more than 22,000 members.

TRANSLATOR'S PREFACE

by Louis J. Puhl, S.J.

Much research has been carried on with regard to *The Spiritual Exercises* of St. Ignatius. The volume on the Exercises in the *Monumenta Historica Societatis Jesu*[1] bears eloquent witness to this. Many years of study have been devoted to investigating whatever concerns this great work. If proof of this is desired, the five volumes of the *Collection de la Bibliothèque des Exercices* afford ample evidence. In the restored Society of Jesus the initiator of this work was Father John Roothaan. By his letters, and by his scholarly translation and commentary on the Exercises, he infused new life into their study. The work has gone on increasing from his day. At present we know more about the Exercises than was known shortly after the death of St. Ignatius. A comparison of a good modern commentary with the Directory would establish this. I fear, however, that our English translations have not kept pace with the progress of modern scholarship in this matter.

There is no dearth of translations into English, all more or less literal.[2]

Such translations have the great advantage of enabling one to see almost at a glance what the original form of expression was. There is less danger, too, in these translations of interpretation and of substituting the translator's ideas for the meaning of the original. Furthermore, emphasis is not so easily shifted to words or phrases in such a way that the meaning is changed.

But these translations also labor under great difficulties, and this seems to be especially true of the Exercises. In this case, a literal translation often fails to render the true meaning, and at times has no meaning at all. The most dangerous source of error is the use of an English word similar to the Spanish and derived from the same

Latin root. Thus *determinar* is translated as "determine," and *afec-ción* as "affection." Even if these English words represent the meaning of similar words in modern Spanish, this may not be true of the language of St. Ignatius. As a result, this practice has been the source of many errors. Words of Latin origin are simply trans-ferred to the translation. Thus the words "annotation," "composi-tion," "election," "deliberation," "deliberate," and others are used, though their meaning does not correspond to the sense in the Span-ish original. The consequence is that a terminology is developed which is not readily understood except by those who are familiar with the Exercises.

The sentence structure and the limping Spanish used by St. Ignatius present even greater difficulties. The modern Spanish sentence is very different from the English sentence, and this is even more true of sixteenth-century Spanish. It is above all true of the Spanish of a Basque nobleman who had only the elements of an education when he wrote his book, and used an acquired language with little knowledge of its literary form. If the long, loosely knit sentences of the Spanish original are retained in English, they make reading and understanding difficult, and turn people from the use and study of the Exercises.

One of the chief difficulties in translation is the constantly recur-ring participial construction. It is vague and not very clear in the original, and becomes impossible in English. It may stand for almost any kind of clause or phrase. To find the correct, corre-sponding English form means interpretation by considering the meaning in the context and in the opinion of the best commenta-tors. Even in modern Spanish, finite forms must be substituted for the constantly recurring gerunds used by St. Ignatius. Frequently, sentences must be broken up, and phrases must be made indepen-dent sentences. The result may appear a very free version, while as a matter of fact it is merely translating clearly and accurately into English.

The aim of this translation is to represent as nearly as possible, idea with idea, Spanish idiom with corresponding English idiom, Spanish sentence structure with English sentence structure, and the quaint forms of the original with the forms common at present.

Every effort has been made to add nothing and to omit nothing.

Idiom may demand frequent omission of connectives where English understands them; accuracy may demand two words to explain one or a circumlocution where no convenient word is available; clearness may demand substituting an equivalent saying or figure for the Spanish where it would not be understood in English. But all these things are required for a correct translation.

The intention is to produce a clear, idiomatic, and readable translation. It is not possible to make a literary translation of a book that is really a set of directions. But by breaking up the long sentences, and by getting away from the Spanish idiom, it is possible to have a translation that can easily be read and understood. Many translations make such difficult reading that those who should be constantly using the book are deterred from doing so.

The text used for the translation is the convenient and accurate Spanish-Latin text, published by Marietti, Turin, 1928, and edited by the author of the critical edition in the volume on the Exercises in the *Monumenta Historica Societatis Jesu.* This edition has convenient marginal numbers for every section, which the editor hopes to make official by inserting in a revision of the critical edition. They prove very useful for cross reference and for gathering material on the Exercises.

Great help has been derived from the excellent German translation of Father Alfred Feder.[3] Since the German language does not use words of Latin origin, the translator does not fall into the error of choosing a word which is similar to the Spanish and derived from the same root, but totally different in meaning. Furthermore, Father Feder has used the latest studies to make his translation accurate.

Another great help was the scholarly edition of the Exercises in Spanish by Father José Calveras, S.J.[4] The discussion in the introduction on the language of Exercises, and the notes giving the modern Spanish equivalents of the expressions and constructions of the Exercises were constantly consulted.

The section on the language of the Exercises, especially the *glossarium* in the volume on the Exercises in the *Monumenta Historica,* also proved very helpful.

The text has been kept clear of all references, and notes arranged according to the marginal numbers have been placed in the back.

They are not a commentary, but state the reasons for the translation adopted and for the form used. Readers long used to Father Roothaan's version and various literal translations may be surprised at the apparent difference between the present text and the traditional renditions. They will find in the notes the reasons for the change.

All of the standard commentaries have influenced the translation, but it is not surprising if the influence of Father Jaime Nonell, S.J., is evident at every turn. For many years his books on the Exercises[5] have been the translator's constant companions, and have been used by him as their clearest and most logical interpretation.

In conclusion the translator wishes to express his thanks for the many valuable suggestions by those who have read the whole manuscript.

Pontifical College Josephinum
Worthington, Ohio

The Spiritual Exercises

SOUL OF CHRIST

Soul of Christ, sanctify me
    Body of Christ, save me
Blood of Christ, inebriate me
    Water from the side of Christ, wash me
Passion of Christ, strengthen me
    O good Jesus, hear me
Within Thy wounds hide me
    Permit me not to be separated from Thee
From the wicked foe defend me
    At the hour of my death call me
And bid me come to Thee
    That with Thy saints I may praise Thee
Forever and ever, Amen.

IHS

INTRODUCTORY OBSERVATIONS

✤

The purpose of these observations is to provide some
understanding of the spiritual exercises which follow
and to serve as a help both for the one who is to give
them and for the exercitant

1. By the term "Spiritual Exercises" is meant every method of examination of conscience, of meditation, of contemplation, of vocal and mental prayer, and of other spiritual activities that will be mentioned later. For just as taking a walk, journeying on foot, and running are bodily exercises, so we call Spiritual Exercises every way of preparing and disposing the soul to rid itself of all inordinate attachments, and, after their removal, of seeking and finding the will of God in the disposition of our life for the salvation of our soul.

2. The one who explains to another the method and order of meditating or contemplating should narrate accurately the facts of the contemplation or meditation. Let him adhere to the points, and add only a short or summary explanation. The reason for this is that when one in meditating takes the solid foundation of facts, and goes over it and reflects on it for himself, he may find something that makes them a little clearer or better understood. This may arise either from his own reasoning, or from the grace of God enlightening his mind. Now this produces greater spiritual relish and fruit than if one in giving the Exercises had explained and developed the meaning at great length. For it is not much knowledge that fills and satisfies the soul, but the intimate understanding and relish of the truth.

3. In all the Spiritual Exercises which follow, we make use of the acts of the intellect in reasoning, and of the acts of the will in manifesting our love. However, we must observe that when in acts of the will we address God our Lord or His saints either vocally or

mentally, greater reverence is required on our part than when we use the intellect in reasoning.

4. Four Weeks are assigned to the Exercises given below. This corresponds to the four parts into which they are divided, namely: the first part, which is devoted to the consideration and contemplation of sin; the second part, which is taken up with the life of Christ our Lord up to Palm Sunday inclusive; the third part, which treats of the passion of Christ our Lord; the fourth part, which deals with the Resurrection and Ascension; to this are appended Three Methods of Prayer.

However, it is not meant that each week should necessarily consist of seven or eight days. For it may happen that in the First Week some are slower in attaining what is sought, namely, contrition, sorrow, and tears for sin. Some, too, may be more diligent than others, and some more disturbed and tried by different spirits. It may be necessary, therefore, at times to shorten the Week, and at others to lengthen it. So in our search for the fruit that is proper to the matter assigned, we may have to do the same in all the subsequent Weeks. However, the Exercises should be finished in approximately thirty days.

5. It will be very profitable for the one who is to go through the Exercises to enter upon them with magnanimity and generosity toward his Creator and Lord, and to offer Him his entire will and liberty, that His Divine Majesty may dispose of him and all he possesses according to His most holy will.

6. When the one who is giving the Exercises perceives that the exercitant is not affected by any spiritual experiences, such as consolations or desolations, and that he is not troubled by different spirits, he ought to ply him with questions about the exercises. He should ask him whether he makes them at the appointed times, and how he makes them. He should question him about the Additional Directions, whether he is diligent in the observance of them. He will demand an account in detail of each one of these points. Consolation and desolation are treated in nos. 316–324; the Additional Directions are given in nos. 73–90.

7. If the director of the Exercises observes that the exercitant is in desolation and tempted, let him not deal severely and harshly with him, but gently and kindly. He should encourage and strengthen him for the future by exposing to him the wiles of the enemy of our human nature, and by getting him to prepare and dispose himself for the coming consolation.

8. If the one who is giving the Exercises should perceive from desolations, from the wiles of the enemy, and from consolations that the exercitant has need of them, he should explain to him the rules of the First Week and of the Second Week for the understanding of different spirits, nos. 313–327, and 328–336.

9. It should be observed that when the exercitant is engaged in the Exercises of the First Week, if he is a person unskilled in spiritual things, and if he is tempted grossly and openly, for example, by bringing before his mind obstacles to his advance in the service of God our Lord, such as labors, shame, fear for his good name in the eyes of the world, etc., the one who is giving the Exercises should not explain to him the rules about different spirits that refer to the Second Week. For while the rules of the First Week will be very helpful to him, those of the Second Week will be harmful, since they deal with matter that is too subtle and advanced for him to understand.

10. When the one who is giving the Exercises perceives that the exercitant is being assailed and tempted under the appearance of good, then is the proper time to explain to him the rules of the Second Week, which we mentioned above. For commonly the enemy of our human nature tempts more under the appearance of good when one is exercising himself in the illuminative way. This corresponds to the Exercises of the Second Week. He does not tempt him so much under the appearance of good when he is exercising himself in the purgative way, which corresponds to the Exercises of the First Week.

11. While the exercitant is engaged in the First Week of the Exercises, it will be helpful if he knows nothing of what is to be done in

the Second Week. Rather, let him labor to attain what he is seeking in the First Week as if he hoped to find no good in the Second.

12. He who is giving the Exercises must insist with the exercitant that since he is to spend an hour in each of the five exercises or contemplations which are made every day, he must always take care that he is satisfied in the consciousness of having persevered in the exercise for a full hour. Let him rather exceed an hour than not use the full time. For the enemy is accustomed to make every effort that the hour to be devoted to a contemplation, meditation, or prayer should be shortened.

13. We must remember that during the time of consolation it is easy, and requires only a slight effort, to continue a whole hour in contemplation, but in time of desolation it is very difficult to do so. Hence, in order to fight against the desolation and conquer the temptation, the exercitant must always remain in the exercise a little more than the full hour. Thus he will accustom himself not only to resist the enemy, but even to overthrow him.

14. If the one who is giving the Exercises sees that the exercitant is going on in consolation and in great fervor, he must admonish him not to be inconsiderate or hasty in making any promise or vow. The more unstable in character he knows him to be, the more he should forewarn and admonish him. For though it is right to urge one to enter the religious state in which he knows that vows of obedience, poverty, and chastity are taken, and though a good work done under vow is more meritorious than one done without a vow, nevertheless, it is necessary to consider with great care the condition and endowments of each individual, and the help or hindrance one would experience in carrying out his promises.

15. The director of the Exercises ought not to urge the exercitant more to poverty or any promise than to the contrary, nor to one state of life or way of living more than to another. Outside the Exercises, it is true, we may lawfully and meritoriously urge all who probably have the required fitness to choose continence, virginity, the religious life, and every form of religious perfection. But while one is engaged in the Spiritual Exercises, it is more suitable and much better that the Creator and Lord in person communicate

Himself to the devout soul in quest of the divine will, that He inflame it with His love and praise, and dispose it for the way in which it could better serve God in the future. Therefore, the director of the Exercises, as a balance at equilibrium, without leaning to one side or the other, should permit the Creator to deal directly with the creature, and the creature directly with his Creator and Lord.

16. Hence, that the Creator and Lord may work with greater certainty in His creature, if the soul chance to be inordinately attached or inclined to anything, it is very proper that it rouse itself by the exertion of all its powers to desire the opposite of that to which it is wrongly attached. Thus if one's attachment leads him to seek and to hold an office or a benefice, not for the honor and glory of God our Lord, nor for the spiritual welfare of souls, but for his own personal gain and temporal interests, he should strive to rouse a desire for the contrary. Let him be insistent in prayer and in his other spiritual exercises in begging God for the reverse, that is, that he neither seek such office or benefice, nor anything else, unless the Divine Majesty duly regulate his desires and change his former attachment. As a result, the reason he wants or retains anything will be solely the service, honor, and glory of the Divine Majesty.

17. While the one who is giving the Exercises should not seek to investigate and know the private thoughts and sins of the exercitant, nevertheless, it will be very helpful if he is kept faithfully informed about the various disturbances and thoughts caused by the action of different spirits. This will enable him to propose some spiritual exercises in accordance with the degree of progress made and suited and adapted to the needs of a soul disturbed in this way.

18. The Spiritual Exercises must be adapted to the condition of the one who is to engage in them, that is, to his age, education, and talent. Thus exercises that he could not easily bear, or from which he would derive no profit, should not be given to one with little natural ability or of little physical strength.

Similarly, each one should be given those exercises that would be more helpful and profitable according to his willingness to dispose himself for them.

Hence, one who wishes no further help than some instruction and the attainment of a certain degree of peace of soul may be given the Particular Examination of Conscience, nos. 24–31, and after that the General Examination of Conscience, nos. 32–43. Along with this, let him be given for half an hour each morning the method of prayer on the Commandments and on the Capital Sins, etc., nos. 238–248. Weekly confession should be recommended to him, and if possible, the reception of Holy Communion every two weeks, or even better, every week if he desires it.

This method is more appropriate for those who have little natural ability or are illiterate. Let each of the Commandments be explained to them, and also the Capital Sins, the use of the five senses, the precepts of the Church, and the Works of Mercy.

Similarly, if the one giving the Exercises sees that the exercitant has little aptitude or little physical strength, that he is one from whom little fruit is to be expected, it is more suitable to give him some of the easier exercises as a preparation for confession. Then he should be given some ways of examining his conscience, and directed to confess more frequently than was his custom before, so as to retain what he has gained.

But let him not go on further and take up the matter dealing with the Choice of a Way of Life, nor any other exercises that are outside the First Week. This is especially to be observed when much better results could be obtained with other persons, and when there is not sufficient time to take everything.

19. One who is educated or talented, but engaged in public affairs or necessary business, should take an hour and a half daily for the Spiritual Exercises.

First, the end for which man is created should be explained to him, then for half an hour the Particular Examination of Conscience may be presented, then the General Examination of Conscience, and the method of confessing and of receiving Holy Communion.

For three days, let him meditate each morning for an hour on the first, second, and third sins, nos. 45–54. For three more days, at the same time, he should take the meditation on personal sins, nos. 55–61. Then for three days, at the same hour, he should meditate on the punishment due to sin, nos. 65–71. Along with all of these meditations, he should be given the ten Additional Directions, nos. 73–89.

In the mysteries of the life of our Lord, the same order should be observed which is explained later on at great length in the Exercises themselves.

20. To one who is more disengaged, and desirous of making as much progress as possible, all the Spiritual Exercises should be given in the same order in which they follow below.

Ordinarily, the progress made in the Exercises will be greater the more the exercitant withdraws from all friends and acquaintances, and from all worldly cares. For example, he can leave the house in which he dwelt and choose another house or room in order to live there in as great privacy as possible, so that he will be free to go to Mass and Vespers every day without any fear that his acquaintances will cause any difficulty.

There are many advantages resulting from this separation, but the following three are the most important:

First, if in order to serve and praise God our Lord one withdraws from numerous friends and acquaintances and from many occupations not undertaken with a pure intention, he gains no little merit before the Divine Majesty.

Secondly, in this seclusion the mind is not engaged in many things, but can give its whole attention to one single interest, that is, to the service of its Creator and its spiritual progress. Thus it is more free to use its natural powers to seek diligently what it so much desires.

Thirdly, the more the soul is in solitude and seclusion, the more fit it renders itself to approach and be united with its Creator and Lord; and the more closely it is united with Him, the more it disposes itself to receive graces and gifts from the infinite goodness of its God.

21.   ## SPIRITUAL EXERCISES
✢
Which have as their purpose the conquest of self and the
regulation of one's life in such a way that no decision is
made under the influence of any inordinate attachment

PRESUPPOSITION

22. To assure better cooperation between the one who is giving the Exercises and the exercitant, and more beneficial results for both, it is necessary to suppose that every good Christian is more ready to put a good interpretation on another's statement than to condemn it as false. If an orthodox construction cannot be put on a proposition, the one who made it should be asked how he understands it. If he is in error, he should be corrected with all kindness. If this does not suffice, all appropriate means should be used to bring him to a correct interpretation, and so defend the proposition from error.

23.   ## FIRST PRINCIPLE AND FOUNDATION

Man is created to praise, reverence, and serve God our Lord, and by this means to save his soul.

The other things on the face of the earth are created for man to help him in attaining the end for which he is created.

Hence, man is to make use of them in as far as they help him in the attainment of his end, and he must rid himself of them in as far as they prove a hindrance to him.

Therefore, we must make ourselves indifferent to all created things, as far as we are allowed free choice and are not under any prohibition. Consequently, as far as we are concerned, we should not prefer health to sickness, riches to poverty, honor to dishonor, a long life to a short life. The same holds for all other things.

Our one desire and choice should be what is more conducive to the end for which we are created.

First Week

24. DAILY PARTICULAR EXAMINATION
OF CONSCIENCE

✤

*There are three different times of the day and two
examinations involved in this practice*

First, in the morning, immediately on rising, one should resolve to guard carefully against the particular sin or defect with regard to which he seeks to correct or improve himself.

25. Secondly, after dinner, he should ask God our Lord for the grace he desires, that is, to recall how often he has fallen into the particular sin or defect, and to avoid it for the future.

Then follows the first examination. He should demand an account of himself with regard to the particular point which he has resolved to watch in order to correct himself and improve. Let him go over the single hours or periods from the time he arose to the hour and moment of the present examination, and in the first line of the figure given below, make a mark for each time that he has fallen into the particular sin or defect. Then he is to renew his resolution, and strive to amend during the time till the second examination is to be made.

26. Thirdly, after supper, he should make a second examination, going over as before each single hour, commencing with the first examination, and going up to the present one. In the second line of the figure given below, let him make a mark for each time he has fallen into the particular fault or sin.

27. FOUR ADDITIONAL DIRECTIONS

✤

*These are to serve as a help to more ready removal of the
particular sin or fault*

1. Every time one falls into the particular sin or fault, let him place his hand upon his breast, and be sorry for having fallen. He

can do this even in the presence of many others without their perceiving what he is doing.

28. 2. Since the first line of the figure to which *G* is prefixed represents the first examination of conscience, and the second one, the second examination, he should observe at night whether there is an improvement from the first line to the second, that is, from the first examination to the second.

29. 3. The second day should be compared with the first, that is, the two examinations of the present day with the two of the preceding day. Let him observe if there is an improvement from one day to another.

30. 4. Let him compare one week with another and observe whether he has improved during the present week as compared with the preceding.

31. *Note*

It should be noted that in the figure below the first *G* is larger, and signifies Sunday. The second is smaller, and stands for Monday, the third for Tuesday, the fourth for Wednesday, and so forth.

32. GENERAL EXAMINATION OF CONSCIENCE

✢

The purpose of this examination of conscience is to
purify the soul and to aid us to improve our confessions

I presuppose that there are three kinds of thoughts in my mind, namely: one which is strictly my own, and arises wholly from my own free will; two others which come from without, the one from the good spirit, and the other from the evil one.

33. Thoughts

There are two ways of meriting from evil thoughts that come from without:

1. When a thought of committing a mortal sin comes to my mind which I resist at once, and thus overcome it.

34. 2. When the same evil thought comes to me, and I resist it, but it returns again and again, and I always resist it till it is conquered.
This second way is more meritorious than the first.

35. It is a venial sin if the same thought of sinning mortally comes to mind and for a short time one pays heed to it, or receives some sense pleasure, or is somewhat negligent in rejecting it.

36. There are two ways of sinning mortally:

1. The first is to consent to the evil thought with the intention of carrying it out, or of doing so if one can.

37. 2. The second way of sinning mortally is actually carrying out the sin to which consent was given.
This is a greater sin for three reasons: 1. Because of the greater duration; 2. Because of the greater intensity; 3. Because of the greater harm done to both persons.

38. Words

(One may also offend God in word in many ways: by blasphemy, by swearing.) One must not swear, neither by the creature nor by the Creator, unless it is according to truth, out of necessity, and with reverence.

By necessity I mean that the truth I swear to is not just some true statement I choose to confirm by oath, but one of real importance, either for the welfare of the soul or of the body, or with regard to temporal interests.

By reverence I mean that when the name of the Creator and Lord is mentioned, one acts with consideration and devoutly manifests due honor and respect.

39. It must be noted that in idle oaths we sin more grievously when we swear by the Creator than when we swear by a creature. However, to swear as one ought, according to truth, out of necessity, with reverence, is more difficult when we swear by a creature than when we swear by the Creator. There are three reasons for this:

1. When we wish to take an oath by some creature, the intention to call upon its name does not make us so attentive and cautious to speak the truth, or to confirm it by oath only if necessary, as we would be with the intention to use the name of the Creator and Lord of all.

2. When we swear by the name of some creature, it is not so easy to observe reverence and respect for the Creator as when in swearing we use the name of the Creator and Lord Himself. For the intention of using the name of God our Lord carries along with it a greater respect and reverence than the intention to use the name of a creature.

Hence, those who are perfect should be allowed to swear by a creature rather than those who are imperfect. The perfect, due to constant contemplation and the enlightenment of the understanding, consider, meditate, and ponder more that God our Lord is in every creature by His essence, power, and presence. Therefore, when they swear by a creature, they are more apt to be disposed to show respect and reverence to the Creator and Lord than those who are imperfect.

3. In frequent swearing by a creature, idolatry is more to be feared in those who are imperfect than in those who are perfect.

40. (Among other sins of the tongue that we must avoid are idle words.) No idle word should be uttered. I understand a word to be

idle when it serves no good purpose, either for myself or for another, and was not intended to do so. Hence, words are never idle when spoken for any useful purpose, or when meant to serve the good of one's own soul or that of another, of the body or of temporal possessions. Nor are they idle because one speaks of matters that do not pertain to his state, for example, if a religious speaks of wars or of commerce. In all we have mentioned, there will be merit if what is said is directed to some good purpose; there will be sin if it is directed to an evil purpose, or if engaged in for no good end.

41. (Lying, false testimony, detraction are also sins of the tongue.) Nothing should be said to lessen the good name of another, or to complain about him. For if I reveal a hidden mortal sin of another, I sin mortally; if I reveal a hidden venial sin, I sin venially; if his defect, I manifest my own.

If, however, my intention is good, there are two ways in which it is permissible to speak of the sin or fault of another:

1. When a sin is public, as in the case of a woman openly leading a shameless life, or of a sentence passed in court, or of a commonly known error that infests the minds of those with whom we live.

2. When a hidden sin is revealed to someone with the intention that he help the one who is in sin to rise from his state. But then there must be some grounds or probable reasons for believing that he will be able to help him.

(Among sins of the tongue may be considered ridicule, insults, and other similar sins, which the one giving the Exercises may discuss if he judges it necessary.)

42. *Deeds*

The subject matter for examination will be the Ten Commandments, the laws of the Church, the recommendations of superiors. All transgressions of obligations arising from any of these three groups are more or less grievous sins according to the gravity of the matter.

By recommendations of superiors is meant crusade indults and other indulgences, such as those for peace on condition of confession and reception of Holy Communion. For to be the cause of one acting against such pious recommendations and regulations of superiors, or to do so oneself, is no small sin.

43.   METHOD OF MAKING THE GENERAL EXAMINATION OF CONSCIENCE

✤

There are five points in this method

1. The first point is to give thanks to God our Lord for the favors received.

2. The second point is to ask for grace to know my sins and to rid myself of them.

3. The third point is to demand an account of my soul from the time of rising up to the present examination. I should go over one hour after another, one period after another. The thoughts should be examined first, then the words, and finally, the deeds in the same order as was explained under the Particular Examination of Conscience.

4. The fourth point will be to ask pardon of God our Lord for my faults.

5. The fifth point will be to resolve to amend with the grace of God. Close with an *Our Father.*

44.   GENERAL CONFESSION AND HOLY COMMUNION

Among many advantages of a general confession which one makes of his own accord during the time of the Spiritual Exercises, there are especially these three:

1. It is true that one who confesses every year has no obligation to make a general confession. But if one is made, there will be

much greater merit and profit, because of the greater sorrow experienced for all the sins and perversities of his whole life.

2. While one is going through the Spiritual Exercises, a far deeper insight into his sins and their malice is acquired than at a time when he is not so engaged with what concerns his inner life. Since at this time he attains to a deeper knowledge and sorrow for his sins, there will be greater profit and merit than he would otherwise have had.

3. As a consequence of having made a better confession, and of being better disposed, he will find that he is more worthy and better prepared to receive the Most Blessed Sacrament. This reception will strengthen him not only against falling into sin, but will also help him to retain the increase of grace which he has gained.

It will be better to make this general confession immediately after the Exercises of the First Week.

45.   **FIRST EXERCISE**

⚜

This is a meditation on the first, second, and third sin
employing the three powers of the soul. After the
preparatory prayer and two preludes it contains three
principal points and a colloquy

46. PRAYER.   In the preparatory prayer I will beg God our Lord for grace that all my intentions, actions, and operations may be directed purely to the praise and service of His Divine Majesty.

47. FIRST PRELUDE.   This is mental representation of the place.
Attention must be called to the following point. When the contemplation or meditation is on something visible, for example, when we contemplate Christ our Lord, the representation will consist in seeing in imagination the material place where the object is that we wish to contemplate. I said the material place, for example, the temple, or the mountain where Jesus or His Mother is, according to the subject matter of the contemplation.
In a case where the subject matter is not visible, as here in a med-

itation on sin, the representation will be to see in imagination my soul as a prisoner in this corruptible body, and to consider my whole composite being as an exile here on earth, cast out to live among brute beasts. I said my whole composite being, body and soul.

48. THE SECOND PRELUDE.   I will ask God our Lord for what I want and desire.

The petition made in this prelude must be according to the subject matter. Thus in a contemplation on the Resurrection I will ask for joy with Christ in joy. In one on the passion, I will ask for sorrow, tears, and anguish with Christ in anguish.

Here it will be to ask for shame and confusion, because I see how many have been lost on account of a single mortal sin, and how many times I have deserved eternal damnation, because of the many grievous sins that I have committed.

49. *Note*

The Preparatory Prayer, which is never changed, and the two Preludes mentioned above, which are changed at times according to the subject matter, must always be made before all the contemplations and meditations.

50. THE FIRST POINT.   This will consist in using the memory to recall the first sin, which was that of the angels, and then in applying the understanding by reasoning upon this sin, then the will by seeking to remember and understand all to be the more filled with shame and confusion when I compare the one sin of the angels with the many sins I have committed. I will consider that they went to hell for one sin, and the number of times I have deserved to be condemned forever because of my numerous sins.

I said we should apply the memory to the sin of the angels, that is, recalling that they were created in the state of grace, that they did not want to make use of the freedom God gave them to reverence and obey their Creator and Lord, and so falling into pride, were changed from grace to hatred of God, and cast out of heaven into hell.

So, too, the understanding is to be used to think over the matter more in detail, and then the will to rouse more deeply the emotions.

51. SECOND POINT.   In the same way the three powers of the soul are to be applied to the sin of Adam and Eve. Recall to memory how on account of this sin they did penance for so long a time, and the great corruption which came upon the human race that caused so many to be lost in hell.

I said recall to mind the second sin, that of our First Parents. After Adam had been created on the Plain of Damascus and placed in the Garden of Paradise, and Eve had been formed from his side, they sinned by violating the command not to eat of the tree of knowledge. Thereafter, they were clothed in garments of skin and cast out of Paradise. By their sin they lost original justice, and for the rest of their lives, lived without it in many labors and great penance.

So, too, the understanding is to be used to think over the matter in greater detail, and the will is to be used as explained above.

52. THIRD POINT.   In like manner, we are to do the same with regard to the third sin, namely, that of one who went to hell because of one mortal sin. Consider also countless others who have been lost for fewer sins than I have committed.

I said to do the same for the third particular sin. Recall to memory the gravity and malice of sin against our Creator and Lord. Use the understanding to consider that because of sin, and of acting against the Infinite Goodness, one is justly condemned forever. Close with the acts of the will as we have said above.

53. COLLOQUY.   Imagine Christ our Lord present before you upon the cross, and begin to speak with him, asking how it is that though He is the Creator, He has stooped to become man, and to pass from eternal life to death here in time, that thus He might die for our sins.

I shall also reflect upon myself and ask:

"What have I done for Christ?"
"What am I doing for Christ?"
"What ought I to do for Christ?"

As I behold Christ in this plight, nailed to the cross, I shall ponder upon what presents itself to my mind.

54. *Note on Colloquies*

The colloquy is made by speaking exactly as one friend speaks to another, or as a servant speaks to a master, now asking him for a favor, now blaming himself for some misdeed, now making known his affairs to him, and seeking advice in them. Close with an *Our Father.*

55. SECOND EXERCISE

✣

This is a meditation on our sins. After the preparatory prayer and two preludes there are five points and a colloquy

PRAYER.   The preparatory prayer will be the same.

FIRST PRELUDE.   This will be the same as in the First Exercise.

SECOND PRELUDE.   This is to ask for what I desire. Here it will be to ask for a growing and intense sorrow and tears for my sins.

56. FIRST POINT.   This is the record of my sins. I will call to mind all the sins of my life, reviewing year by year, and period by period. Three things will help me in this: First, to consider the place where I lived; secondly, my dealings with others; thirdly, the office I have held.

57. SECOND POINT.   I will weigh the gravity of my sins, and see the loathsomeness and malice which every mortal sin I have committed has in itself, even though it were not forbidden.

58. THIRD POINT.   I will consider who I am, and by means of examples humble myself:

1. What am I compared with all men?

2. What are all men compared with the angels and saints of paradise?

3. Consider what all creation is in comparison with God. Then I alone, what can I be?

4. I will consider all the corruption and loathsomeness of my body.

5. I will consider myself as a source of corruption and contagion from which has issued countless sins and evils and the most offensive poison.

59. FOURTH POINT. I will consider who God is against whom I have sinned, going through His attributes and comparing them with their contraries in me: His wisdom with my ignorance, His power with my weakness, His justice with my iniquity, His goodness with my wickedness.

60. FIFTH POINT. This is a cry of wonder accompanied by surging emotion as I pass in review all creatures. How is it that they have permitted me to live, and have sustained me in life! Why have the angels, though they are the sword of God's justice, tolerated me, guarded me, and prayed for me! Why have the saints interceded for me and asked favors for me! And the heavens, sun, moon, stars, and the elements; the fruits, birds, fishes, and other animals—why have they all been at my service! How is it that the earth did not open to swallow me up, and create new hells in which I should be tormented forever!

61. COLLOQUY. I will conclude with a colloquy, extolling the mercy of God our Lord, pouring out my thoughts to Him, and giving thanks to Him that up to this very moment He has granted me life. I will resolve with His grace to amend for the future. Close with an *Our Father.*

62. ### THIRD EXERCISE

✛

*This is a repetition of the first and second exercises with
three colloquies*

After the preparatory prayer and the two preludes, this exercise will consist in repeating the First and Second Exercise. In doing this, we should pay attention to and dwell upon those points in which we have experienced greater consolation or desolation or greater spiritual appreciation. After the repetition, three colloquies are to be used in the following manner:

63. FIRST COLLOQUY.   The first colloquy will be with our Blessed Lady, that she may obtain grace for me from her Son and Lord for three favors:

    1. A deep knowledge of my sins and a feeling of abhorrence for them;

    2. An understanding of the disorder of my actions, that filled with horror of them, I may amend my life and put it in order;

    3. A knowledge of the world, that filled with horror, I may put away from me all that is worldly and vain.
    Then I will say a *Hail Mary.*

SECOND COLLOQUY.   I will make the same petitions to her Son that He may obtain these graces from the Father for me.
    After that I will say *Soul of Christ.*

THIRD COLLOQUY.   I will make the same requests of the Father that He Himself, the eternal Lord, may grant them to me.
    Then I will close with the *Our Father.*

64.   **FOURTH EXERCISE**

                    ✣

This exercise consists of a summary of the third exercise
given above

I have called it a summary, because the intellect, without any digression, diligently thinks over and recalls the matter contemplated in the previous exercises. The same three colloquies should be used at the close.

65.   FIFTH EXERCISE

✣

This is a meditation on hell. Besides the preparatory
prayer and two preludes it contains five points and a
colloquy.

PRAYER.   The preparatory prayer will be as usual.

FIRST PRELUDE.   This is a representation of the place. Here it will
be to see in imagination the length, breadth, and depth of hell.

SECOND PRELUDE.   I should ask for what I desire. Here it will be to
beg for a deep sense of the pain which the lost suffer, that if because
of my faults I forget the love of the eternal Lord, at least the fear of
these punishments will keep me from falling into sin.

66. FIRST POINT.   This will be to see in imagination the vast fires,
and the souls enclosed, as it were, in bodies of fire.

67. SECOND POINT.   To hear the wailing, the howling, cries, and
blasphemies against Christ our Lord and against His saints.

68. THIRD POINT.   With the sense of smell to perceive the smoke,
the sulphur, the filth, and corruption.

69. FOURTH POINT.   To taste the bitterness of tears, sadness, and
remorse of conscience.

70. FIFTH POINT.   With the sense of touch to feel the flames which
envelop and burn the souls.

71. COLLOQUY.   Enter into conversation with Christ our Lord.
Recall to memory that of those who are in hell, some came there
because they did not believe in the coming of Christ; others, though
they believed, because they did not keep the Commandments.
Divide them all into three classes:

    1. Those who were lost before the coming of Christ;

    2. Those who were lost during His lifetime;

    3. Those who were lost after His life here on earth.

Thereupon, I will give thanks to God our Lord that He has not put an end to my life and permitted me to fall into any of these three classes.

I shall also thank Him for this, that up to this very moment He has shown Himself so loving and merciful to me.

Close with an *Our Father.*

(OTHER EXERCISES)

(If the one giving the Exercises judges that it would be profitable for the exercitant, other exercises may be added here, for example, on death and other punishments of sin, on judgment, etc. Let him not think this is forbidden, though they are not given here.)

72. *Note*

The First Exercise will be made at midnight; the Second, immediately on rising in the morning; the Third, before or after Mass, at all events before dinner; the Fourth, about the time of Vespers; the Fifth, an hour before supper.

This is more or less the arrangement of hours that I take for granted is being observed in all four Weeks. But as age, condition of health, and the physical constitution of the exercitant permit, there may be five exercises or fewer.

73.   ADDITIONAL DIRECTIONS
                            ✢
          *The purpose of these directions is to help one to go
        through the exercises better and find more readily what
                            he desires*

  1. After retiring, just before falling asleep, for the space of a *Hail Mary,* I will think of the hour when I have to rise, and why I am rising, and briefly sum up the exercise I have to go through.

74. 2. When I wake up, I will not permit my thoughts to roam at random, but will turn my mind at once to the subject I am about to

contemplate in the first exercise at midnight. I will seek to rouse myself to shame for my many sins by using examples, let us say, of a knight brought before his king and the whole court, filled with shame and confusion for having grievously offended his lord from whom he had formerly received many gifts and favors. Similarly, in the Second Exercise, I will consider myself a great sinner, loaded with chains, that is, I will look upon myself as bound with fetters, going to appear before the supreme and eternal Judge, and I will recall the way prisoners, bound and deserving of death, appear before an earthly judge. As I dress, I will think over these thoughts or others in keeping with the subject matter of the meditation.

75. 3. I will stand for the space of an *Our Father,* a step or two before the place where I am to meditate or contemplate, and with my mind raised on high, consider that God our Lord beholds me, etc. Then I will make an act of reverence or humility.

76. 4. I will enter upon the meditation, now kneeling, now prostrate upon the ground, now lying face upwards, now seated, now standing, always being intent on seeking what I desire. Hence, two things should be noted:

1. If I find what I desire while kneeling, I will not seek to change my position: if prostrate, I will observe the same direction, etc.

2. I will remain quietly meditating upon the point in which I have found what I desire, without any eagerness to go on till I have been satisfied.

77. 5. After an exercise is finished, either sitting or walking, I will consider for the space of a quarter of an hour how I succeeded in the meditation or contemplation. If poorly, I will seek the cause of the failure; and after I have found it, I will be sorry, so that I may do better in the future. If I have succeeded, I will give thanks to God our Lord, and the next time try to follow the same method.

78. 6. I should not think of things that give pleasure and joy, as the glory of heaven, the Resurrection, etc., for if I wish to feel pain, sorrow, and tears for my sins, every consideration promoting joy and happiness will impede it. I should rather keep in mind that I want

to be sorry and feel pain. Hence it would be better to call to mind death and judgment.

79. 7. For the same reason I should deprive myself of all light, closing the shutters and doors when I am in my room, except when I need light to say prayers, to read, or to eat.

80. 8. I should not laugh or say anything that would cause laughter.

81. 9. I should restrain my eyes except to look up in receiving or dismissing one with whom I have to speak.

PENANCE

82. 10. The tenth Additional Direction deals with penance. This is divided into interior and exterior penance. Interior penance consists in sorrow for one's sins and a firm purpose not to commit them or any others. Exterior penance is the fruit of the first kind. It consists in inflicting punishment on ourselves for the sins we have committed. The principal ways of doing this are three:

83. 1. The first kind of exterior penance concerns eating. In this matter, if we do away with what is superfluous, it is not penance, but temperance. We do penance when we deny ourselves something of what is suitable for us. The more we do this, the better the penance, provided only we do no harm to ourselves and do not cause any serious illness.

84. 2. The second kind of exterior penance concerns sleep. Here, too, it is not penance when we do away with the superfluous in what is pampering and soft. But it is penance when in our manner of sleeping we take something away from what is suitable. The more we do in this line, the better it is, provided we do not cause any harm to ourselves, and do not bring on any notable illness. But we should not deny ourselves a suitable amount of sleep, except to come to a happy mean in case we had the habit of sleeping too much.

85. 3. The third kind of penance is to chastise the body, that is, to inflict sensible pain on it. This is done by wearing hairshirts, cords, or iron chains on the body, or by scourging or wounding oneself, and by other kinds of austerities.

86. THE MORE SUITABLE AND SAFE FORM OF PENANCE SEEMS TO BE that which would cause sensible pain to the body and not penetrate to the bones, so that it inflicts pain, but does not cause sickness. For this reason it would seem more suitable to chastise oneself with light cords that cause superficial pain, rather than in any other way that might bring about a serious internal infirmity.

NOTES

87. NOTE I. The principal reason for performing exterior penance is to secure three effects:

1. To make satisfaction for past sins;

2. To overcome oneself, that is, to make our sensual nature obey reason, and to bring all of our lower faculties into greater subjection to the higher;

3. To obtain some grace or gift that one earnestly desires. Thus it may be that one wants a deep sorrow for sin, or tears, either because of his sins or because of the pains and sufferings of Christ our Lord; or he may want the solution of some doubt that is in his mind.

88. NOTE II. Note that the first and second Additional Directions are to be observed for the exercises at midnight and at daybreak, and not for the exercises made at other times. The fourth Direction is never to be followed in the church before others, but only in private, for example, at home.

89. NOTE III. When the exercitant has not found what he has been seeking, for example, tears, consolation, etc., it is often useful to make some change in the kind of penance, such as in food, in

sleep, or in other ways of doing penance, so that we alternate, for two or three days doing penance, and for two or three not doing any. The reason for this is that more penance is better for some and less for others. Another reason is that we often quit doing penance, because we are too much concerned about our bodies and erroneously judge that human nature cannot bear it without notable illness. On the other hand, at times we may do too much penance, thinking that the body can stand it. Now since God our Lord knows our nature infinitely better, when we make changes of this kind, He often grants each one the grace to understand what is suitable for him.

90. NOTE IV.   The Particular Examination of Conscience will be made to remove faults and negligences with regard to the Exercises and the Additional Directions. This will also be observed in the Second, Third, and Fourth Weeks.

The Kingdom of Christ

THE CALL OF AN EARTHLY KING

❧

*This will help us to contemplate
the life of the eternal king*

PRAYER. The preparatory prayer will be as usual.

FIRST PRELUDE. This is a mental representation of the place. Here it will be to see in imagination the synagogues, villages, and towns where Christ our Lord preached.

SECOND PRELUDE. I will ask for the grace I desire. Here it will be to ask of our Lord the grace not to be deaf to His call, but prompt and diligent to accomplish His most holy will.

FIRST PART

92. FIRST POINT. This will be to place before my mind a human king, chosen by God our Lord Himself, to whom all Christian princes and people pay homage and obedience.

93. SECOND POINT. This will be to consider the address this king makes to all his subjects, with the words: "It is my will to conquer all the lands of the infidel. Therefore, whoever wishes to join with me in this enterprise must be content with the same food, drink, clothing, etc., as mine. So, too, he must work with me by day, and watch with me by night, etc., that as he has had a share in the toil with me, afterwards, he may share in the victory with me."

94. THIRD POINT. Consider what the answer of good subjects ought to be to a king so generous and noble-minded, and consequently, if anyone would refuse the invitation of such a king, how justly he would deserve to be condemned by the whole world, and looked upon as an ignoble knight.

SECOND PART

95. The second part of this exercise will consist in applying the example of the earthly king mentioned above to Christ our Lord according to the following points:

FIRST POINT.   If such a summons of an earthly king to his subjects deserves our attention, how much more worthy of consideration is Christ our Lord, the Eternal King, before whom is assembled the whole world. To all His summons goes forth, and to each one in particular He addresses the words: "It is my will to conquer the whole world and all my enemies, and thus to enter into the glory of my Father. Therefore, whoever wishes to join me in this enterprise must be willing to labor with me, that by following me in suffering, he may follow me in glory."

96. SECOND POINT.   Consider that all persons who have judgment and reason will offer themselves entirely for this work.

97. THIRD POINT.   Those who wish to give greater proof of their love, and to distinguish themselves in whatever concerns the service of the eternal King and the Lord of all, will not only offer themselves entirely for the work, but will act against their sensuality and carnal and worldly love, and make offerings of greater value and of more importance in words such as these:

98.   **ETERNAL LORD OF ALL THINGS**

✳

*Eternal Lord of all things, in the presence of Thy
infinite goodness, and of Thy glorious mother, and of all
the saints of Thy heavenly court, this is the offering of
myself which I make with Thy favor and help. I protest
that it is my earnest desire and my deliberate choice,
provided only it is for Thy greater service and praise, to
imitate Thee in bearing all wrongs and all abuse and all
poverty, both actual and spiritual, should Thy most holy
majesty deign to choose and admit me to such a state and
way of life*

NOTES

99. NOTE I.   This exercise should be gone through twice during the day, that is, in the morning on rising, and an hour before dinner, or before supper.

100. NOTE II.   During the Second Week and thereafter, it will be very profitable to read some passages from the *Following of Christ,* or from the Gospels, and from the *Lives of the Saints.*

Second Week

FIRST DAY AND
FIRST CONTEMPLATION

✤

This is a contemplation on the incarnation. After the preparatory prayer and three preludes there are three points and a colloquy

PRAYER.   The usual preparatory prayer.

102. FIRST PRELUDE.   This will consist in calling to mind the history of the subject I have to contemplate. Here it will be how the Three Divine Persons look down upon the whole expanse or circuit of all the earth, filled with human beings. Since They see that all are going down to hell, They decree in Their eternity that the Second Person should become man to save the human race. So when the fullness of time had come, They send the Angel Gabriel to our Lady. Cf. no. 262.

103. SECOND PRELUDE.   This is a mental representation of the place. It will be here to see the great extent of the surface of the earth, inhabited by so many different peoples, and especially to see the house and room of our Lady in the city of Nazareth in the province of Galilee.

104. THIRD PRELUDE.   This is to ask for what I desire. Here it will be to ask for an intimate knowledge of our Lord, who has become man for me, that I may love Him more and follow Him more closely.

105. *Note*

Attention must be called to the following point. The same preparatory prayer without any change, as was mentioned in the beginning, and the three preludes, with such changes of form as the subject demands, are to be made during this Week and during the others that follow.

106. FIRST POINT.   This will be to see the different persons:
First, those on the face of the earth, in such great diversity in dress and in manner of acting. Some are white, some black; some at

peace, and some at war; some weeping, some laughing; some well, some sick; some coming into the world, and some dying; etc.

Secondly, I will see and consider the Three Divine Persons seated on the royal dais or throne of the Divine Majesty. They look down upon the whole surface of the earth, and behold all nations in great blindness, going down to death and descending into hell.

Thirdly, I will see our Lady and the angel saluting her.

I will reflect upon this to draw profit from what I see.

107. SECOND POINT.   This will be to listen to what the persons on the face of the earth say, that is, how they speak to one another, swear and blaspheme, etc. I will also hear what the Divine Persons say, that is, "Let us work the redemption of the human race," etc. Then I will listen to what the angel and our Lady say. Finally, I will reflect upon all I hear to draw profit from their words.

108. THIRD POINT.   This will be to consider what the persons on the face of the earth do, for example, wound, kill, and go down to hell. Also what the Divine Persons do, namely, work the most holy Incarnation, etc. Likewise, what the Angel and our Lady do; how the Angel carries out his office of ambassador; and how our Lady humbles herself, and offers thanks to the Divine Majesty.

Then I shall reflect upon all to draw some fruit from each of these details.

109. COLLOQUY.   The exercise should be closed with a colloquy. I will think over what I ought to say to the Three Divine Persons, or to the eternal Word incarnate, or to His Mother, our Lady. According to the light that I have received, I will beg for grace to follow and imitate more closely our Lord, who has just become man for me.

Close with an *Our Father.*

110.   THE SECOND CONTEMPLATION

✙

The Nativity

PRAYER.   The usual preparatory prayer.

111. FIRST PRELUDE. This is the history of the mystery. Here it will be that our Lady, about nine months with child, and, as may be piously believed, seated on an ass, set out from Nazareth. She was accompanied by Joseph and a maid, who was leading an ox. They are going to Bethlehem to pay the tribute that Caesar imposed on those lands. Cf. no. 264.

112. SECOND PRELUDE. This is a mental representation of the place. It will consist here in seeing in imagination the way from Nazareth to Bethlehem. Consider its length, its breadth; whether level, or through valleys and over hills. Observe also the place or cave where Christ is born; whether big or little; whether high or low; and how it is arranged.

113. THIRD PRELUDE. This will be the same as in the preceding contemplation and identical in form with it.

114. FIRST POINT. This will consist in seeing the persons, namely, our Lady, St. Joseph, the maid, and the Child Jesus after His birth. I will make myself a poor little unworthy slave, and as though present, look upon them, contemplate them, and serve them in their needs with all possible homage and reverence.

Then I will reflect on myself that I may reap some fruit.

115. SECOND POINT. This is to consider, observe, and contemplate what the persons are saying, and then to reflect on myself and draw some fruit from it.

116. THIRD POINT. This will be to see and consider what they are doing, for example, making the journey and laboring that our Lord might be born in extreme poverty, and that after many labors, after hunger, thirst, heat, and cold, after insults and outrages, He might die on the cross, and all this for me.

Then I will reflect and draw some spiritual fruit from what I have seen.

117. COLLOQUY. Close with a colloquy as in the preceding contemplation, and with the *Our Father.*

118.   THE THIRD CONTEMPLATION

✣

This will be a repetition of the first and second exercises

After the preparatory prayer and the three preludes, a repetition of the First and Second Exercises will be made. In doing this, attention should always be given to some more important parts in which one has experienced understanding, consolation, or desolation.

Close the exercise with a colloquy and an *Our Father.*

119. In this repetition and in all those which follow, the same order of proceeding should be observed as in the repetitions of the First Week. The subject matter is changed but the same form is observed.

120.   THE FOURTH CONTEMPLATION

✣

*This will consist in a repetition of the first and second
exercises in the same way as in the repetition given
above*

121.   THE FIFTH CONTEMPLATION

✣

*This will consist in applying the five senses to the matter
of the first and second contemplations*

After the preparatory prayer and three preludes, it will be profitable with the aid of the imagination to apply the five senses to the subject matter of the First and Second Contemplations in the following manner:

122. FIRST POINT.   This consists in seeing in imagination the persons, and in contemplating and meditating in detail the circumstances in which they are, and then in drawing some fruit from what has been seen.

123. SECOND POINT. This is to hear what they are saying, or what they might say, and then by reflecting on oneself to draw some profit from what has been heard.

124. THIRD POINT. This is to smell the infinite fragrance, and taste the infinite sweetness of the divinity. Likewise to apply these senses to the soul and its virtues, and to all according to the person we are contemplating, and to draw fruit from this.

125. FOURTH POINT. This is to apply the sense of touch, for example, by embracing and kissing the place where the persons stand or are seated, always taking care to draw some fruit from this.

126. COLLOQUY. Conclude with a colloquy and with an *Our Father* as in the First and Second Contemplations.

NOTES

127. NOTE I. Attention must be called to the following point. Throughout this Week and the subsequent Weeks, I ought to read only the mystery that I am immediately to contemplate. Hence, I should not read any mystery that is not to be used on that day or at that hour, lest the consideration of one mystery interfere with the contemplation of the other.

128. NOTE II. The First Exercise on the Incarnation should take place at midnight, the second at daybreak, the third about the time of Mass, the fourth near the time of Vespers, and the fifth an hour before supper.

The same order should be observed on all the following days.

129. NOTE III. If the exercitant is old or weak, or even when strong, if he has come from the First Week rather exhausted, it should be noted that in this Second Week it would be better, at least at times, not to rise at midnight. Then one contemplation would be in the morning, another would be at the time of Mass, a third before dinner, with one repetition of them at the time of Vespers, and the Application of the Senses before supper.

130. NOTE IV. Of the ten Additional Directions given during the First Week, the following should be changed during the Second Week: the second, the sixth, the seventh, and part of the tenth.

The second will be that as soon as I awake, I should place before my mind the subject of the contemplation with the desire to know better the eternal Word Incarnate in order to serve and follow Him more closely.

The sixth will be to call to mind frequently the mysteries of the life of Christ our Lord from the Incarnation to the place or mystery I am contemplating.

The seventh will be that the exercitant take care to darken his room, or admit the light; to make use of pleasant or disagreeable weather, in as far as he perceives that it may be of profit, and help to find what he desires.

In the observance of the tenth Additional Direction, the exercitant must conduct himself as the mysteries he is contemplating demand. Some call for penance; others do not.

Thus all ten Additional Directions are to be observed with great care.

131. NOTE V. In all the exercises, except the one at midnight and the one in the morning, an equivalent of the second Additional Direction should be observed as follows:

As soon as I recall that it is time for the exercise in which I ought to engage, before proceeding to it, I will call to mind where I am going, before whom I am to appear, and briefly sum up the exercise. Then after observing the third Additional Direction, I shall enter upon the exercise.

132.   SECOND DAY

On the second day, for the first and second contemplations, the Presentation in the Temple, no. 268, and the Flight into Exile in Egypt, no. 269, should be used. Two repetitions will be made of these contemplations, and the Application of the Senses, in the same way as was done on the preceding day.

133. *Note*

Sometimes it will be profitable, even when the exercitant is strong and well-disposed, to make some changes from the second day to the fourth inclusive in order to attain better what is desired. Thus, the first contemplation would be the one on rising. Then there would be a second about the time of Mass, a repetition about the time of Vespers, and the Application of the Senses before supper.

134.   **THIRD DAY**

On the third day use the contemplations on the Obedience of the Child Jesus to His parents, no. 271, and the Finding of the Child Jesus in the Temple, no. 272. Then will follow the two repetitions and the Application of the Senses.

135.   **INTRODUCTION TO THE
         CONSIDERATION OF DIFFERENT
              STATES OF LIFE**

The example which Christ our Lord gave of the first state of life, which is that of observing the Commandments, has already been considered in meditating on His obedience to His parents. The example of the second state, which is that of evangelical perfection, has also been considered, when He remained in the temple and left His foster father and His Mother to devote Himself exclusively to the service of His eternal Father.

While continuing to contemplate His life, let us begin to investigate and ask in what kind of life or in what state His Divine Majesty wishes to make use of us.

Therefore, as some introduction to this, in the next exercise, let us consider the intention of Christ our Lord, and on the other hand, that of the enemy of our human nature. Let us also see how we ought to prepare ourselves to arrive at perfection in whatever state or way of life God our Lord may grant us to choose.

136.   THE FOURTH DAY
A MEDITATION ON TWO STANDARDS

✣

The one of Christ, our supreme leader and lord, the
other of Lucifer, the deadly enemy of our human nature

PRAYER.   The usual preparatory prayer.

137. FIRST PRELUDE.   This is the history. Here it will be that Christ
calls and wants all beneath His standard, and Lucifer, on the other
hand, wants all under his.

138. SECOND PRELUDE.   This is a mental representation of the
place. It will be here to see a great plain, comprising the whole
region about Jerusalem, where the sovereign Commander-in-
Chief of all the good is Christ our Lord; and another plain about
the region of Babylon, where the chief of the enemy is Lucifer.

139. THIRD PRELUDE.   This is to ask for what I desire. Here it will
be to ask for a knowledge of the deceits of the rebel chief and help
to guard myself against them; and also to ask for a knowledge of
the true life exemplified in the sovereign and true Commander,
and the grace to imitate Him.

FIRST PART

THE STANDARD OF SATAN

140. FIRST POINT.   Imagine you see the chief of all the enemy in
the vast plain about Babylon, seated on a great throne of fire and
smoke, his appearance inspiring horror and terror.

141. SECOND POINT.   Consider how he summons innumerable
demons, and scatters them, some to one city and some to another,
throughout the whole world, so that no province, no place, no state
of life, no individual is overlooked.

142. THIRD POINT.   Consider the address he makes to them, how
he goads them on to lay snares for men and bind them with chains.
First they are to tempt them to covet riches (as Satan himself is

accustomed to do in most cases) that they may the more easily attain the empty honors of this world, and then come to overweening pride.

The first step, then, will be riches, the second honor, the third pride. From these three steps the evil one leads to all other vices.

Second Part

THE STANDARD OF CHRIST

143. In a similar way, we are to picture to ourselves the sovereign and true Commander, Christ our Lord.

144. First Point. Consider Christ our Lord, standing in a lowly place in a great plain about the region of Jerusalem, His appearance beautiful and attractive.

145. Second Point. Consider how the Lord of all the world chooses so many persons, apostles, disciples, etc., and sends them throughout the whole world to spread His sacred doctrine among all men, no matter what their state or condition.

146. Third Point. Consider the address which Christ our Lord makes to all His servants and friends whom He sends on this enterprise, recommending to them to seek to help all, first by attracting them to the highest spiritual poverty, and should it please the Divine Majesty, and should He deign to choose them for it, even to actual poverty. Secondly, they should lead them to a desire for insults and contempt, for from these springs humility.

Hence, there will be three steps: the first, poverty as opposed to riches; the second, insults or contempt as opposed to the honor of this world; the third, humility as opposed to pride. From these three steps, let them lead men to all other virtues.

147. Colloquy. A colloquy should be addressed to our Lady, asking her to obtain for me from her Son and Lord the grace to be received under His standard, first in the highest spiritual poverty, and should the Divine Majesty be pleased thereby, and deign to choose and accept me, even in actual poverty; secondly, in bearing

insults and wrongs, thereby to imitate Him better, provided only I can suffer these without sin on the part of another, and without offense of the Divine Majesty. Then I will say the *Hail Mary.*

SECOND COLLOQUY.   This will be to ask her Son to obtain the same favors for me from the Father. Then I will say, *Soul of Christ.*

THIRD COLLOQUY.   This will be to beg the Father to grant me the same graces. Then I will say the *Our Father.*

148. *Note*

This exercise will be made at midnight and again in the morning. There will be two repetitions of the same exercise, one about the time of Mass and the other about the time of Vespers. The same three colloquies, with our Lady, with her Son, and with the Father, will close all these exercises as well as the one on the Three Classes of Men, which follows an hour before supper.

149.   **THREE CLASSES OF MEN**

✤

*This is a meditation for the same fourth day to choose
that which is better*

PRAYER.   The usual preparatory prayer.

150. FIRST PRELUDE.   This is the history of the Three Classes of Men. Each of them has acquired ten thousand ducats, but not entirely as they should have, for the love of God. They all wish to save their souls and find peace in God our Lord by ridding themselves of the burden arising from the attachment to the sum acquired, which impedes the attainment of this end.

151. SECOND PRELUDE.   This is a mental representation of the place. Here it will be to behold myself standing in the presence of God our Lord and of all His saints, that I may know and desire what is more pleasing to His Divine Goodness.

152. THIRD PRELUDE.   This is to ask for what I desire. Here it will be to beg for the grace to choose what is more for the glory of His Divine Majesty and the salvation of my soul.

153. THE FIRST CLASS.   They would like to rid themselves of the attachment they have to the sum acquired in order to find peace in God our Lord and assure their salvation, but the hour of death comes, and they have not made use of any means.

154. THE SECOND CLASS.   They want to rid themselves of the attachment, but they wish to do so in such a way that they retain what they have acquired, so that God is to come to what they desire, and they do not decide to give up the sum of money in order to go to God, though this would be the better way for them.

155. THE THIRD CLASS.   These want to rid themselves of the attachment, but they wish to do so in such a way that they desire neither to retain nor to relinquish the sum acquired. They seek only to will and not will as God our Lord inspires them, and as seems better for the service and praise of the Divine Majesty. Meanwhile, they will strive to conduct themselves as if every attachment to it had been broken. They will make efforts neither to want that, nor anything else, unless the service of God our Lord alone move them to do so. As a result, the desire to be better able to serve God our Lord will be the cause of their accepting anything or relinquishing it.

156. THREEFOLD COLLOQUY.   I will make use of the same three colloquies employed in the preceding contemplation on Two Standards.

157. *Note*

It should be noted that when we feel an attachment opposed to actual poverty or a repugnance to it, when we are not indifferent to poverty and riches, it will be very helpful in order to overcome the inordinate attachment, even though corrupt nature rebel against it, to beg our Lord in the colloquies to choose us to serve Him in actual poverty. We should insist that we desire it, beg for it, plead for it, provided, of course, that it be for the service and praise of the Divine Goodness.

158.   FIFTH DAY

The contemplation on the journey of Christ our Lord from
Nazareth to the river Jordan and His baptism. Cf. no. 273.

NOTES

159. NOTE I.   This matter should be contemplated once at midnight, and again in the morning. There will be two repetitions of it,
one about the time of Mass and the other about the time of Vespers.
Before supper there will be the Application of the Senses to the
same mystery.

In each of these five exercises, there will be at the beginning the
preparatory prayer and the three preludes as was fully explained in
the contemplations on the Incarnation and the Nativity. They will
conclude with the three colloquies of the meditation on Three
Classes of Men, or according to the note which follows this meditation.

160. NOTE II.   The Particular Examination of Conscience after
dinner and after supper will be made upon the faults and negligences with regard to the exercises of the day and on the Additional Directions. The same will be observed on the subsequent
days.

161.   SIXTH DAY

The contemplation will be on Christ our Lord's departure from the
river Jordan for the desert and on the temptations. The same directions that were given for the fifth day will be followed here.

SEVENTH DAY

St. Andrew and others follow Christ our Lord. Cf. no. 275.

EIGHTH DAY

The Sermon on the Mount, which is on the eight beatitudes, cf. no. 278.

NINTH DAY

Christ our Lord appears to His disciples on the waves of the sea. Cf. no. 280.

TENTH DAY

Our Lord preaches in the temple. Cf. no. 288.

ELEVENTH DAY

The raising of Lazarus, cf. no. 285.

TWELFTH DAY

Palm Sunday, cf. no. 287.

NOTES

162. NOTE I.   Everyone, according to the time he wishes to devote to the contemplations of this Second Week, and according to his progress, may lengthen or shorten this Week.

If he wishes to lengthen it, let him take the mysteries of the Visitation of our Lady to Elizabeth, the Shepherds, the Circumcision of the Child Jesus, the Three Kings, and also others.

If he wishes to shorten the Week, he may omit even some of the mysteries that have been assigned. For they serve here to afford an introduction and method for better and more complete meditation later.

163. NOTE II. The treatment of the matter dealing with the Choice of a Way of Life will begin with the contemplation of our Lord's departure from Nazareth for the Jordan, taken inclusively, that is, on the Fifth Day, as is explained later.

164. NOTE III. Before entering upon the Choice of a Way of Life, in order that we may be filled with love of the true doctrine of Christ our Lord, it will be very useful to consider attentively the following Three Kinds of Humility. These should be thought over from time to time during the whole day, and the three colloquies should also be added as will be indicated further on.

THREE KINDS OF HUMILITY

165. THE FIRST KIND OF HUMILITY. This is necessary for salvation. It consists in this, that as far as possible I so subject and humble myself as to obey the law of God our Lord in all things, so that not even were I made lord of all creation, or to save my life here on earth, would I consent to violate a commandment, whether divine or human, that binds me under pain of mortal sin.

166. THE SECOND KIND OF HUMILITY. This is more perfect than the first. I possess it if my attitude of mind is such that I neither desire nor am I inclined to have riches rather than poverty, to seek honor rather than dishonor, to desire a long life rather than a short life, provided only in either alternative I would promote equally the service of God our Lord and the salvation of my soul. Besides this indifference, this second kind of humility supposes that not for all creation, nor to save my life, would I consent to commit a venial sin.

167. THE THIRD KIND OF HUMILITY. This is the most perfect kind of humility. It consists in this. If we suppose the first and second kind attained, then whenever the praise and glory of the Divine Majesty would be equally served, in order to imitate and be

in reality more like Christ our Lord, I desire and choose poverty with Christ poor, rather than riches; insults with Christ loaded with them, rather than honors; I desire to be accounted as worthless and a fool for Christ, rather than to be esteemed as wise and prudent in this world. So Christ was treated before me.

168. *Note*

If one desires to attain this third kind of humility, it will help very much to use the three colloquies at the close of the meditation on the three Classes of Men mentioned above. He should beg our Lord to deign to choose him for this third kind of humility, which is higher and better, that he may the more imitate and serve Him, provided equal or greater praise and service be given to the Divine Majesty.

169.   INTRODUCTION TO MAKING A CHOICE OF A WAY OF LIFE

In every good choice, as far as depends on us, our intention must be simple. I must consider only the end for which I am created, that is, for the praise of God our Lord and for the salvation of my soul. Hence, whatever I choose must help me to this end for which I am created.

I must not subject and fit the end to the means, but the means to the end. Many first choose marriage, which is a means, and secondarily the service of God our Lord in marriage, though the service of God is the end. So also others first choose to have benefices, and afterwards to serve God in them. Such persons do not go directly to God, but want God to conform wholly to their inordinate attachments. Consequently, they make of the end a means, and of the means an end. As a result, what they ought to seek first, they seek last.

Therefore, my first aim should be to seek to serve God, which is the end, and only after that, if it is more profitable, to have a benefice or marry, for these are means to the end. Nothing must move me to use such means, or to deprive myself of them, save only the service and praise of God our Lord, and the salvation of my soul.

170.   MATTERS ABOUT WHICH
A CHOICE SHOULD BE MADE

✣

*The purpose of this consideration is to afford
information on the matters about which a choice should
be made. It contains four points and a note*

FIRST POINT.   It is necessary that all matters of which we wish to make a choice be either indifferent or good in themselves, and such that they are lawful within our Holy Mother, the hierarchical Church, and not bad or opposed to her.

171. SECOND POINT.   There are things that fall under an unchangeable choice, such as the priesthood, marriage, etc. There are others with regard to which our choice may be changed, for example, to accept or relinquish a benefice, to receive or renounce temporal goods.

172. THIRD POINT.   With regard to an unchangeable choice, once it has been made, for instance, by marriage or the priesthood, etc., since it cannot be undone, no further choice is possible. Only this is to be noted. If the choice has not been made as it should have been, and with due order, that is, if it was not made without inordinate attachments, one should be sorry for this, and take care to live well in the life he has chosen.

Since such a choice was inordinate and awry, it does not seem to be a vocation from God, as many erroneously believe. They make a divine call out of a perverse and wicked choice. For every vocation that comes from God is always pure and undefiled, uninfluenced by the flesh or any inordinate attachment.

173. FOURTH POINT.   In matters that may be changed, if one has made a choice properly and with due order, without any yielding to the flesh or the world, there seems to be no reason why he should make it over. But let him perfect himself as much as possible in the one he has made.

174. *Note*

It is to be observed that if a choice in matters that are subject to change has not been made sincerely and with due order, then, if one desires to bring forth fruit that is worthwhile and most pleasing in the sight of God our Lord, it will be profitable to make a choice in the proper way.

175. ## THREE TIMES WHEN A CORRECT
AND GOOD CHOICE OF A WAY
OF LIFE MAY BE MADE

FIRST TIME.   When God our Lord so moves and attracts the will that a devout soul without hesitation, or the possibility of hesitation, follows what has been manifested to it. St. Paul and St. Matthew acted thus in following Christ our Lord.

176. SECOND TIME.   When much light and understanding are derived through experience of desolations and consolations and discernment of diverse spirits.

177. THIRD TIME.   This is a time of tranquillity. One considers first for what purpose man is born, that is, for the praise of God our Lord and for the salvation of his soul. With the desire to attain this before his mind, he chooses as a means to this end a kind of life or state within the bounds of the Church that will be a help in the service of his Lord and for the salvation of his soul.

I said it is a time of tranquillity, that is, a time when the soul is not agitated by different spirits, and has free and peaceful use of its natural powers.

178. If a choice of a way of life has not been made in the first and second time, below are given:

TWO WAYS OF MAKING A CHOICE OF A WAY OF LIFE IN THE THIRD TIME

FIRST WAY OF MAKING A GOOD AND CORRECT CHOICE OF A WAY OF LIFE

✳

This contains six points

FIRST POINT.   This is to place before my mind the object with regard to which I wish to make a choice, for example, an office, or the reception or rejection of a benefice, or anything else that may be the object of a choice subject to change.

179. SECOND POINT.   It is necessary to keep as my aim the end for which I am created, that is, the praise of God our Lord and the salvation of my soul. Besides this, I must be indifferent, without any inordinate attachment, so that I am not more inclined or disposed to accept the object in question than to relinquish it, nor to give it up than to accept it. I should be like a balance at equilibrium, without leaning to either side, that I might be ready to follow whatever I perceive is more for the glory and praise of God our Lord and for the salvation of my soul.

180. THIRD POINT.   I should beg God our Lord to deign to move my will, and to bring to my mind what I ought to do in this matter that would be more for His praise and glory. Then I should use the understanding to weigh the matter with care and fidelity, and make my choice in conformity with what would be more pleasing to His most holy will.

181. FOURTH POINT.   This will be to weigh the matter by reckoning the number of advantages and benefits that would accrue to me if I had the proposed office or benefice solely for the praise of God our Lord and the salvation of my soul. On the other hand, I should weigh the disadvantages and dangers there might be in having it. I will do the same with the second alternative, that is, weigh the advantages and benefits as well as the disadvantages and danger of not having it.

182. FIFTH POINT. After I have gone over and pondered in this way every aspect of the matter in question, I will consider which alternative appears more reasonable. Then I must come to a decision in the matter under deliberation because of weightier motives presented to my reason, and not because of any sensual inclination.

183. SIXTH POINT. After such a choice or decision, the one who has made it must turn with great diligence to prayer in the presence of God our Lord, and offer Him his choice that the Divine Majesty may deign to accept and confirm it if it is for His greater service and praise.

184.

SECOND WAY OF MAKING A
CORRECT AND GOOD CHOICE
OF A WAY OF LIFE

✤

This contains four rules and a note

FIRST RULE. The love that moves and causes one to choose must descend from above, that is, from the love of God, so that before one chooses he should perceive that the greater or less attachment for the object of his choice is solely because of His Creator and Lord.

185. SECOND RULE. I should represent to myself a man whom I have never seen or known, and whom I would like to see practice all perfection. Then I should consider what I would tell him to do and choose for the greater glory of God our Lord and the greater perfection of his soul. I will do the same, and keep the rule I propose to others.

186. THIRD RULE. This is to consider what procedure and norm of action I would wish to have followed in making the present choice if I were at the moment of death. I will guide myself by this and make my decision entirely in conformity with it.

187. FOURTH RULE. Let me picture and consider myself as standing in the presence of my judge on the last day, and reflect what decision in the present matter I would then wish to have made. I

will choose now the rule of life that I would then wish to have observed, that on the day of judgment I may be filled with happiness and joy.

188. *Note*

Guided by the rules given above for my eternal salvation and peace, I will make my decision, and will offer it to God our Lord as directed in the sixth point of the First Way of Making a Choice of a Way of Life.

189.   DIRECTIONS FOR THE
          AMENDMENT AND REFORMATION
          OF ONE'S WAY OF LIVING IN
          HIS STATE OF LIFE

It must be borne in mind that some may be established in an ecclesiastical office, or may be married, and hence cannot make a choice of a state of life, or, in matters that may be changed and hence are subject to a choice, they may not be very willing to make one.

It will be very profitable for such persons, whether they possess great wealth or not, in place of a choice, to propose a way for each to reform his manner of living in his state by setting before him the purpose of his creation and of his life and position, namely, the glory and praise of God our Lord and the salvation of his soul.

If he is really to attain this end, during the Exercises and during the consideration of the ways of making a choice as explained above, he will have to examine and weigh in all its details how large a household he should maintain, how he ought to rule and govern it, how he ought to teach its members by word and example. So too he should consider what part of his means should be used for his family and household, how much should be set aside for distribution to the poor and other pious purposes.

Let him desire and seek nothing except the greater praise and glory of God our Lord as the aim of all he does. For everyone must keep in mind that in all that concerns the spiritual life his progress will be in proportion to his surrender of self-love and of his own will and interests.

Third Week

THE FIRST CONTEMPLATION AT MIDNIGHT

✤

Christ our Lord goes from Bethany to Jerusalem and the
Last Supper. No. 289. It contains the preparatory prayer,
three preludes, six points, and a colloquy

PRAYER.   The usual preparatory prayer.

191. FIRST PRELUDE.   This is the history. Here it will be to recall that Christ our Lord sent two of His disciples from Bethany to Jerusalem to prepare the Supper, and afterwards, He himself went there with His disciples. After they had eaten the Paschal Lamb and supped, He washed their feet, and gave His most Sacred Body and Precious Blood to His disciples When Judas had gone out to sell his Lord, Christ addressed His disciples.

192. SECOND PRELUDE.   This is a mental representation of the place. Here it will be to consider the way from Bethany to Jerusalem, whether narrow or broad, whether level, etc.; also the place of the Supper, whether great or small, whether of this or that appearance.

193. THIRD PRELUDE.   This is to ask for what I desire. Here it will be to ask for sorrow, compassion, and shame because the Lord is going to His suffering for my sins.

194. FIRST POINT.   This is to see the persons at the Supper, and to reflect upon myself, and strive to draw some profit from them.

SECOND POINT. This is to listen to their conversation, and likewise seek to draw fruit from it.

THIRD POINT. This is to see what they are doing, and to seek to draw some fruit from it.

195. FOURTH POINT.   This will be to consider what Christ our Lord suffers in His human nature, or according to the passage contemplated, what he desires to suffer. Then I will begin with great effort to strive to grieve, be sad, and weep. In this way I will labor through all the points that follow.

196. FIFTH POINT.   This is to consider how the divinity hides itself; for example, it could destroy its enemies and does not do so, but leaves the most sacred humanity to suffer so cruelly.

197. SIXTH POINT.   This is to consider that Christ suffers all this for my sins, and what I ought to do and suffer for Him.

198. COLLOQUY.   Close with a colloquy to Christ our Lord, and at the end, say the *Our Father.*

199. *Note*

Attention must be called to the following point which was mentioned before and in part explained. In the colloquy, one should talk over motives and present petitions according to circumstances. Thus he may be tempted or he may enjoy consolation, may desire to have this virtue or another, may want to dispose himself in this or that way, may seek to grieve or rejoice according to the matter that he is contemplating. Finally, he should ask what he more earnestly desires with regard to some particular interests.

Following this advice, he may engage in only one colloquy with Christ our Lord, or, if the matter and his devotion prompt him to do so, he may use three colloquies, one with the Mother of our Lord, one with her Son, and one with the Father. If three colloquies are used, the same form should be followed that was given in the meditation on Two Standards, and the note that follows after the Three Classes of Men should be observed.

200.   SECOND CONTEMPLATION
                              ✤
            *In the morning. From the Last Supper to the Agony in
                        the Garden inclusive*

PRAYER.   The usual preparatory prayer.

201. FIRST PRELUDE.   This is the history of the mystery. Here it
will be as follows: Christ our Lord descended with the eleven disciples from Mt. Sion, where the Supper was held, to the Valley of Josaphat. Eight of the disciples were left at a place in the valley, and
the other three in a part of the garden. Then Jesus began His
prayer, and His sweat became as drops of blood. Three times He
prayed to His Father and went to rouse His disciples from sleep.
After His enemies had fallen to the ground at His word, and Judas
had given Him the kiss, after St. Peter had cut off the ear of
Malchus, and Christ had healed it, Jesus was seized as a malefactor,
and led down through the valley and again up the slope to the
house of Annas.

202. SECOND PRELUDE.   This is to see the place. It will be here to
consider the way from Mt. Sion to the Valley of Josaphat, likewise
the garden, its breadth, its length, and appearance.

203. THIRD PRELUDE.   This is to ask for what I desire. In the Passion it is proper to ask for sorrow with Christ in sorrow, anguish
with Christ in anguish, tears and deep grief because of the great
affliction Christ endures for me.

                              NOTES

204. NOTE I.   In this second contemplation, after the preparatory
prayer and the three preludes given above, the same way of proceeding in the points and colloquies is to be observed as was followed in the first contemplation on the Supper.
    About the time of Mass and Vespers, two repetitions are to be
made of the first and second contemplations. Before supper the
Application of the Senses should be made on the subject matter of

the two contemplations. The preparatory prayer, and the preludes, adapted to the subject of the exercise, are always to precede. The form to be observed is the same as that given and explained in the Second Week.

205. NOTE II.   As far as age, health, and physical constitution permit the exercitant to do so, he will use five exercises each day, or fewer.

206. NOTE III.   In the Third Week some modification of the second and sixth Additional Directions is necessary.

The second will be that as soon as I awake I will call to mind where I am going and the purpose. I will briefly summarize the contemplation on which I am about to enter. According to the subject matter, I will make an effort while rising and dressing to be sad and grieve because of the great sorrow and suffering of Christ our Lord.

The sixth Additional Direction will be changed as follows. I will take care not to bring up pleasing thoughts, even though they are good and holy, for example, of the Resurrection and the glory of heaven. Rather I will rouse myself to sorrow, suffering, and anguish by frequently calling to mind the labors, fatigue, and suffering which Christ our Lord endured from the time of His birth down to the mystery of the passion upon which I am engaged at present.

207. NOTE IV.   The Particular Examination of Conscience should be made on the Exercises and the Additional Directions as applied to this Week, as was done in the past Week.

208.   SECOND DAY

At midnight the contemplation will be on the events from the Garden to the house of Annas inclusive. Cf. no. 291.

In the morning, from the house of Annas to the house of Caiphas inclusive. Cf. no. 292.

There will be two repetitions and the Application of the Senses as explained above.

THIRD DAY

At midnight, from the house of Caiphas to the house of Pilate inclusive. Cf. no. 293.

In the morning, from Pilate to Herod inclusive. Cf. no. 294.

Then the repetitions and the Application of the Senses in the same way as has been noted.

FOURTH DAY

At midnight, from Herod to Pilate, no. 295, using for this contemplation only the first half of what occurred in the house of Pilate, and afterwards in the morning, the remaining part.

There will be the two repetitions and the Application of the Senses as explained.

FIFTH DAY

At midnight, from the house of Pilate to the Crucifixion, no. 296, and in the morning, from the raising of the cross to His death, no. 297.

Thereafter the repetitions and the Application of the Senses.

SIXTH DAY

At midnight from the taking down from the cross to the burial exclusive, no. 298, and in the morning from the burial inclusive to the house to which our Lady retired after the burial of her Son.

SEVENTH DAY

The contemplation of the whole passion in one exercise at midnight, and again in the morning.

In place of the two repetitions and the Application of the Senses, one should consider as frequently as possible throughout this whole day that the most Sacred Body of Christ our Lord remained separated from the soul, and the place and manner of burial. Let him consider, likewise, the desolation of our Lady, her great sorrow and weariness, and also that of the disciples.

209. *Note*

If one wishes to spend more time on the passion, he should use fewer mysteries in each contemplation, thus, in the first, only the Supper; in the second, only the washing of feet; in the third, the institution of the Blessed Sacrament; in the fourth, Christ's parting address, and so on for the other contemplations and mysteries.

In like manner, after the passion is finished, he may devote one whole day to the consideration of the first half of the passion, and a second day to the other half, and a third day to the whole passion.

On the other hand, if he should wish to spend less time on the passion, he may take the Supper at midnight, the Agony in the Garden in the morning; about the time of Mass, Jesus before Annas; about the time of Vespers, Jesus before Caiphas; and instead of the Application of the Senses at the hour before supper, Jesus before Pilate. In this way, without repetitions or Applications of the Senses, there should be five exercises each day, using for each one a distinct mystery of the life of Christ our Lord. After he has finished the whole passion in this way, he may use another day to go through the entire passion, either in one exercise or in several, as is deemed best for his greater profit.

210.   RULES WITH REGARD TO EATING

✤

To secure for the future due order in the use of food

First Rule. There is less need of abstinence from bread, since it is not a food concerning which the appetite is wont to be so inordinate and temptation so insistent as with other kinds of food.

211. SECOND RULE.   As to drink, abstinence seems to be more necessary than in eating bread. Hence, one should consider carefully
what would be helpful, and therefore to be permitted; and what
would be harmful, and to be avoided.

212. THIRD RULE.   As to foods, greater and more complete abstinence is to be observed. For with regard to them the appetite tends
more readily to be excessive, and temptation to be insistent. To
avoid disorder concerning foods, abstinence may be practiced in
two ways:
    First, by accustoming oneself to eat coarser foods;
    Secondly, if delicacies are taken, to eat of them only sparingly.

213. FOURTH RULE.   Provided care is taken not to fall sick, the
more one retrenches from a sufficient diet, the more speedily he
will arrive at the mean he should observe in the matter of food and
drink. There are two reasons for this:
    First, by thus using the means to dispose himself, he will often
experience more abundantly within the soul lights, consolations,
and divine inspirations by which the proper mean will become evident to him.
    Secondly, if he perceives that with such abstinence he has not
sufficient strength and health for the Spiritual Exercises, he will
easily come to understand what is more suitable to sustain his body.

214. FIFTH RULE.   While one is eating, let him imagine he sees
Christ our Lord and His disciples at table, and consider how He
eats and drinks, how He looks, how He speaks, and then strive to
imitate Him. In this way, his mind will be occupied principally
with our Lord, and less with the provision for the body. Thus he
will come to greater harmony and order in the way he ought to
conduct himself.

215. SIXTH RULE. While eating, one may also occupy himself
with some other consideration, either of the life of the saints, or of
some pious reflection, or of a spiritual work he has on hand. For
when a person is attentive to anything of this kind, there will be less
sensible gratification in the nourishment of the body.

216. Seventh Rule.   Above all, let him be on his guard against being wholly intent upon what he is eating, and against being carried away by his appetite so as to eat hurriedly. Let him always be master of himself, both in the manner of eating and in the amount he eats.

217. Eighth Rule.   To do away with what is inordinate, it will be very helpful after dinner or after supper, or at any time when one does not feel a desire for food, to arrange for the next dinner or supper, and so every day to fix the amount that is proper for him to eat. Let him not exceed this, no matter what his appetite or the temptation. Rather, to overcome better every disorderly appetite and temptation of the enemy, if he is tempted to eat more, let him eat less.

Fourth Week

218.   FIRST CONTEMPLATION

✤

The apparition of Christ our Lord to our Lady. No. 299

PRAYER.   The usual preparatory prayer.

219. FIRST PRELUDE.   This is the history. Here it is how after Christ expired on the cross His body remained separated from the soul, but always united with the divinity. His soul, likewise united with the divinity, descended into hell. There he sets free the souls of the just, then comes to the sepulcher, and rising, appears in body and soul to His Blessed Mother.

220. SECOND PRELUDE.   This is a mental representation of the place. Here it will be to see the arrangement of the holy sepulcher and the place or house of our Lady. I will note its different parts, and also her room, her oratory, etc.

221. THIRD PRELUDE.   This will be to ask for what I desire. Here it will be to ask for the grace to be glad and rejoice intensely because of the great joy and the glory of Christ our Lord.

222. THE FIRST, SECOND, AND THIRD POINTS.   These will be the usual ones as presented in the contemplation on the Last Supper.

223. FOURTH POINT.   This will be to consider the divinity, which seemed to hide itself during the passion, now appearing and manifesting itself so miraculously in the most holy Resurrection in its true and most sacred effects.

224. FIFTH POINT.   Consider the office of consoler that Christ our Lord exercises, and compare it with the way in which friends are wont to console each other.

225. COLLOQUY.   Close with a colloquy, or colloquies, as the circumstances suggest, and at the end say the *Our Father.*

NOTES

226. NOTE I.   In the subsequent contemplations, all the mysteries from the Resurrection to the Ascension inclusive are to be gone through in the manner indicated below. As for the rest, throughout the whole Week of the Resurrection, let the same form be used and the same method observed as were followed during the entire Week devoted to the passion.

The first contemplation on the Resurrection, given above, will serve as a guide. The preludes will be the same, but adapted to the matter being considered. The five points will be the same. The Additional Directions will be as given below. In all the rest, for example, with regard to the repetitions, the Application of the Senses, the shortening or lengthening of the mysteries, etc., the Week devoted to the passion may serve as a model.

227. NOTE II.   Ordinarily, it is more in keeping with this Week than with those that have passed to have four exercises a day instead of five.

In that case the first will be on rising in the morning, the second about the time of Mass, or before dinner, in place of the first repetition. The third, about the time of Vespers, will be in place of the second repetition. The fourth, before supper, will be the Application of the Senses to the matter of the three contemplations of the day.

In making the Application of the Senses, attention and more time is to be given to the more important parts and to points where the soul was more deeply moved and spiritual relish was greater.

228. NOTE III.   Though in all the contemplations a definite number of points is given, say three, or five, etc., the one who is contemplating may make use of more or fewer as seems better for him. For this reason it will be very useful before entering on the contemplation to foresee and determine a definite number of points that are to be used.

229. NOTE IV.   In the Fourth Week a change is to be made in the second, sixth, seventh, and tenth Additional Directions.

The second will be, as soon as I awake, to place before my mind the contemplation I am to enter upon, and then to strive to feel joy and happiness at the great joy and happiness of Christ our Lord.

The sixth will be to call to mind and think on what causes pleasure, happiness, and spiritual joy, for instance, the glory of heaven.

The seventh will be, as far as there is reason to believe that it
might help us to rejoice in our Creator and Redeemer, to make use
of the light and the pleasures of the seasons, for example, in sum-
mer of the refreshing coolness, in the winter of the sun and fire.

The tenth will be, instead of penance, to attend to temperance
and moderation in all, except on days of fast and abstinence
ordained by the Church, which must always be observed if there is
no legitimate excuse.

Contemplation
to Attain Love of God

230.

CONTEMPLATION TO ATTAIN
THE LOVE OF GOD

NOTE.   Before presenting this exercise it will be good to call attention to two points:

   1.   The first is that love ought to manifest itself in deeds rather than in words.

231. 2. The second is that love consists in a mutual sharing of goods, for example, the lover gives and shares with the beloved what he possesses, or something of that which he has or is able to give; and vice versa, the beloved shares with the lover. Hence, if one has knowledge, he shares it with the one who does not possess it; and so also if one has honors, or riches. Thus, one always gives to the other.

PRAYER.   The usual prayer.

232. FIRST PRELUDE.   This is the representation of the place, which here is to behold myself standing in the presence of God our Lord and of His angels and saints, who intercede for me.

233. SECOND PRELUDE.   This is to ask for what I desire. Here it will be to ask for an intimate knowledge of the many blessings received, that filled with gratitude for all, I may in all things love and serve the Divine Majesty.

234. FIRST POINT.   This is to recall to mind the blessings of creation and redemption, and the special favors I have received.
   I will ponder with great affection how much God our Lord has done for me, and how much He has given me of what He possesses, and finally, how much, as far as He can, the same Lord desires to give Himself to me according to His divine decrees.
   Then I will reflect upon myself, and consider, according to all reason and justice, what I ought to offer the Divine Majesty, that is, all I possess and myself with it. Thus, as one would do who is moved by great feeling, I will make this offering of myself:

TAKE, LORD, AND RECEIVE

✤

Take, Lord, and receive all my liberty, my memory, my understanding, and my entire will, all that I have and possess. Thou hast given all to me. To Thee, O Lord, I return it. All is Thine, dispose of it wholly according to Thy will. Give me Thy love and Thy grace, for this is sufficient for me.

235. SECOND POINT.   This is to reflect how God dwells in creatures: in the elements giving them existence, in the plants giving them life, in the animals conferring upon them sensation, in man bestowing understanding. So He dwells in me and gives me being, life, sensation, intelligence; and makes a temple of me, since I am created in the likeness and image of the Divine Majesty.

Then I will reflect upon myself again in the manner stated in the first point, or in some other way that may seem better.

The same should be observed with regard to each of the points given below.

236. THIRD POINT.   This is to consider how God works and labors for me in all creatures upon the face of the earth, that is, He conducts Himself as one who labors. Thus, in the heavens, the elements, the plants, the fruits, the cattle, etc., He gives being, conserves them, confers life and sensation, etc.

Then I will reflect on myself.

237. FOURTH POINT.   This is to consider all blessings and gifts as descending from above. Thus, my limited power comes from the supreme and infinite power above, and so, too, justice, goodness, mercy, etc., descend from above as the rays of light descend from the sun, and as the waters flow from their fountains, etc.

Then I will reflect on myself, as has been said.

Conclude with a colloquy and the *Our Father.*

Three Methods of Prayer

THE FIRST METHOD OF PRAYER

The First Method of Prayer is on the Ten Commandments, the Seven Capital Sins, the three powers of the soul, and the five senses.

   This manner of praying is not meant so much to provide a form and method of prayer properly so called, but rather to supply a way of proceeding and some practices by which the soul may prepare itself and profit so that its prayer may be acceptable to God.

I. ON THE TEN COMMANDMENTS

239. ADDITIONAL DIRECTION.   First an equivalent of the second Additional Direction as given in the Second Week is to be observed, that is, before entering on the prayer I recollect myself for a while, and either seated or walking up and down, as may seem better, I will consider where I am going, and for what purpose. The same direction should be observed at the beginning of all the methods of prayer.

240. PRAYER.   A preparatory prayer should be made, for example, I ask God our Lord for grace to know how I have failed in the observance of the Ten Commandments, and also for grace and help to amend for the future. I will beg for a perfect understanding of them in order to observe them better and glorify and praise the Divine Majesty more.

241. METHOD.   In this first method of prayer I should consider and think over the First Commandment, asking myself how I have observed it, and in what I have failed. I will use as a measure of this consideration the space of time it takes to recite three times the *Our Father* and the *Hail Mary*. If during this time I find faults I have committed, I will ask forgiveness and say an *Our Father*. This same method will be followed with each of the Ten Commandments.

NOTES

242. NOTE I.   If one comes to the consideration of a Commandment against which he is not in the habit of committing any sins, it is not necessary to delay so long on it. According as he finds that he sins more or less against a Commandment, he should devote more or less time to the examination and consideration of it. The same rule should be observed with regard to the Capital Sins.

243. NOTE II.   After one has finished the consideration of all the Commandments as indicated above, and has accused himself of his faults, and asked for grace and help to amend for the future, he should close with a colloquy to God our Lord, adapted to the subject matter.

244.   ## II. ON THE CAPITAL SINS

METHOD.   With regard to the Seven Capital Sins, after the Additional Direction, the preparatory prayer should be made in the way prescribed, but with the modification that the object is the sins to be avoided, whereas before, it was the Commandments to be observed. In like manner the method prescribed, the regulation of the time, and the colloquy are to be observed.

245. NOTE.   In order to understand better the faults committed that come under the Seven Capital Sins, let the contrary virtues be considered. So also, the better to avoid these sins, one should resolve to endeavor by devout exercises to acquire and retain the seven virtues contrary to them.

246.   ## III. ON THE THREE POWERS
                        OF THE SOUL

METHOD.   With regard to the three powers of the soul, observe the same method, measure of time, and additional direction as for the Commandments. As there, use a preparatory prayer and colloquy.

247.   IV. ON THE FIVE SENSES
                              OF THE BODY

METHOD.   With regard to the five senses of the body, the same
method should always be observed, only the subject matter is
changed.

248. NOTE.   If anyone wishes to imitate Christ our Lord in the use
of the senses, he should recommend himself to His Divine Majesty
in the preparatory prayer, and after the consideration of each sense
say a *Hail Mary* or an *Our Father.*

If he wishes to imitate our Lady in the use of his senses, he
should recommend himself to her in the preparatory prayer that
she obtain for him this grace from her Son and Lord, and after the
consideration of each sense say a *Hail Mary.*

249.   SECOND METHOD OF PRAYER

                              ✢

           This consists in contemplating the meaning of each
                         word of a prayer

250. ADDITIONAL DIRECTION.   The same Additional Direction
used in the First Method of Prayer should be used here also.

251. PREPARATORY PRAYER.   This should be made according to the
person to whom the prayer is addressed.

252. METHOD.   This is as follows: One may kneel or sit, as may be
better suited to his disposition and more conducive to devotion. He
should keep his eyes closed, or fixed in one position without per-
mitting them to roam. Then let him say, "Father," and continue
meditating upon this word as long as he finds various meanings,
comparisons, relish, and consolation in the consideration of it. The
same method should be followed with each word of the *Our Father,*
or of any other prayer which he wishes to use for this method.

253. RULE I.   He should continue for an hour in the way
described, going through the whole *Our Father.* When he has fin-

ished, let him say the *Hail Mary,* the *Creed, Soul of Christ,* and *Hail Holy Queen,* vocally or mentally, in the usual way.

254. RULE II.   If in contemplation, say on the *Our Father,* he finds in one or two words abundant matter for thought and much relish and consolation, he should not be anxious to go on, though the whole hour be taken up with what he has found. When the hour is over, let him say the rest of the *Our Father* in the usual way.

255. RULE III.   If he has been occupied with one or two words of the *Our Father* for a whole hour, when he wishes to pray on another day, let him say those words in the ordinary way, and commence to contemplate as stated in the second rule with the words that follow immediately after them.

256. NOTE I.   After one or more days, when he has finished the *Our Father,* he should use the *Hail Mary* for prayer in the same way, then other forms of prayer, so that for some time he is always engaged with one of them.

257. NOTE II.   At the end of the prayer, he should turn to the person to whom the prayer is directed, and in a few words ask for the virtues or graces which he sees he needs most.

258.   THIRD METHOD OF PRAYER

A MEASURED RHYTHMICAL RECITATION

ADDITIONAL DIRECTION.   The same Additional Direction will be observed here as in the First and Second Methods.

PRAYER.   The preparatory prayer will be as in the Second Method of Prayer.

METHOD.   This is as follows: With each breath or respiration, one should pray mentally while saying a single word of the *Our Father,* or other prayer that is being recited, in such a way that from one breath to another a single word is said. For this same space of time, the attention is chiefly directed to the meaning of the word, to the person who is addressed, to our own lowliness, or the difference between the greatness of the person and our own littleness. In this way, observing the same measure of time, he should go through the other words of the *Our Father.* Let the other prayers, the *Hail Mary,* the *Soul of Christ,* the *Creed,* and the *Hail Holy Queen,* be recited in the ordinary way.

259. Rule I.   On another day, or at some other time, when he wishes to pray, he may recite the *Hail Mary* in this measured rhythm, and the other prayers in the ordinary way.

260. Rule II.   He who wishes to spend more time in this measured prayer may say all the prayers mentioned above, or a part of them in this way. But let him keep the same method of a breath for the measure as has been explained above.

The Mysteries of the Life of Our Lord

261.

THE MYSTERIES OF THE
LIFE OF OUR LORD

NOTE. In all the mysteries given below, all the words that are in quotation marks are from the Gospel itself, but not those that are outside the quotation marks. Usually three points are given in order to make it easier to meditate and contemplate on the mysteries.

262.

THE ANNUNCIATION TO OUR LADY

✤

St. Luke 1, 26–38

FIRST POINT. The angel, St. Gabriel, salutes our Lady, and announces to her the conception of Christ our Lord: "He went in unto her and said, 'Hail full of grace . . . Thou shalt conceive in the womb and bring forth a son.' "

SECOND POINT. The angel confirms what he had said to her by announcing to her the conception of St. John the Baptist: "And behold Elizabeth thy kinswoman, she also has conceived a son in her old age."

THIRD POINT. Our Lady replied to the angel: "Behold the handmaid of the Lord; be it done unto me according to thy word."

263.

THE VISITATION OF OUR LADY
TO ELIZABETH

✤

St. Luke 1, 39–56

FIRST POINT. When our Lady visited Elizabeth, St. John the Baptist in his mother's womb knew the visit of our Lady. "And it came to pass that when Elizabeth heard the salutation of Mary, the babe in her womb leapt and Elizabeth was filled with the Holy Spirit, and she lifted up her voice with a loud cry and said, 'Blessed art thou among women and blessed is the fruit of thy womb.' "

SECOND POINT.   Our Lady chants the *Magnificat,* saying, "My soul doth magnify the Lord."

THIRD POINT.   "Mary stayed with her about three months, and returned to her own home."

264.   BIRTH OF CHRIST OUR LORD

✣

St. Luke 2, 1–14

FIRST POINT.   Our Lady and her spouse Joseph go from Nazareth to Bethlehem. "Joseph also went up from Galilee to Bethlehem to profess his subjection to Caesar with Mary his espoused wife who was with child."

SECOND POINT.   "She brought forth her first-born son and she swathed him round and laid him in a manger."

THIRD POINT.   "There appeared with the angel a great multitude of the heavenly host praising God and saying, 'Glory to God in the highest.'"

265.   THE SHEPHERDS

✣

St. Luke 2, 8–20

FIRST POINT.   The birth of Christ our Lord was made known to the shepherds by the angel: "I bring to you glad tidings of great joy . . . for there has been born to you this day a Savior."

SECOND POINT.   The shepherds go to Bethlehem. "They went with haste and found Mary and Joseph and the babe lying in the manger."

THIRD POINT.   "The shepherds returned glorifying and praising God."

266.   THE CIRCUMCISION

✣

St. Luke 2, 21

FIRST POINT.   They circumcised the Child Jesus.

SECOND POINT.   "His name was called Jesus, whereby he was called by the angel before he was conceived in the womb."

THIRD POINT.   They returned the Child to His Mother who felt compassion for Him because of the blood He shed.

267.   THE MAGI

✣

St. Matthew 2, 1–12

FIRST POINT.   The Three Kings, Magi, guided by the star came to adore Jesus, saying, "We have seen his star in the East and have come to adore him."

SECOND POINT.   They adore Him and offer Him gifts, "And falling down they worshipped him . . . and offered him gifts, gold, frankincense, and myrrh."

THIRD POINT.   "Being warned in a dream not to return to Herod, they withdrew to their own country by another way."

268.   THE PURIFICATION OF OUR LADY
          AND THE PRESENTATION OF
               THE CHILD JESUS

✣

St. Luke 2, 22–39

FIRST POINT.   They take the Child Jesus to the temple to be offered as the firstborn to the Lord, and they offer for him "a pair of turtle doves or two young pigeons."

SECOND POINT. Coming into the temple, Simeon received Him into his arms saying, "Now thou dost dismiss, O Master, thy servant in peace."

THIRD POINT. Anna "came upon them and gave thanks to God, and spoke of the Child to all who were awaiting the redemption of Jerusalem."

269. THE FLIGHT INTO EGYPT
✢
St. Matthew 2, 13–18

FIRST POINT. Herod wished to kill the Child Jesus and so killed the Innocents, but before their deaths the angel warned Joseph that he should flee: "Arise, take the child and his mother and flee into Egypt."

SECOND POINT. He withdrew into Egypt: "So he arose...by night and withdrew into Egypt."

THIRD POINT. "There he remained till the death of Herod."

270. THE RETURN FROM EGYPT
✢
St. Matthew 2, 19–23

FIRST POINT. The angel admonished Joseph to return to Israel: "Arise, take the child and his mother and go into the land of Israel."

SECOND POINT. "He arose...and came into the land of Israel."

THIRD POINT. "Since Archelaus, the son of Herod, ruled in Judea, he withdrew to Nazareth."

271.   THE LIFE OF CHRIST OUR LORD
                 FROM THE AGE OF TWELVE
                   TO THE AGE OF THIRTY

                              ✣

                      St. Luke 2, 51–52

FIRST POINT.   He was obedient to His parents.

SECOND POINT.   "Jesus advanced in wisdom and age and grace."

THIRD POINT.   He appears to have practiced the trade of a carpenter, as St. Mark seems to show in chapter six: "Is not this the carpenter?"

272.   JESUS GOES UP TO THE
            TEMPLE AT THE AGE OF TWELVE

                              ✣

                      St. Luke 2, 41–50

FIRST POINT.   Christ our Lord at the age of twelve years goes up from Nazareth to Jerusalem.

SECOND POINT.   Christ our Lord remained in Jerusalem, and His parents did not know it.

THIRD POINT.   After three days they found him disputing in the temple, and seated in the midst of the doctors, and when they asked Him where he had been, He answered, "Know you not that I needs must be about my Father's business?"

273.   THE BAPTISM OF CHRIST

                              ✣

                      St. Matthew 3, 13–17

FIRST POINT.   After Christ our Lord had bidden farewell to His blessed Mother, He went from Nazareth to the River Jordan where St. John the Baptist was.

SECOND POINT. St. John baptized Christ our Lord. When he wished to excuse himself because he thought himself unworthy to baptize Him, our Lord said to him: "Let it be so at this time; for so it becometh to fulfill all justness."

THIRD POINT. The Holy Spirit descended upon Him, and the voice of the Father from heaven testified, "This is my beloved Son in whom I am well pleased."

274. THE TEMPTATION OF CHRIST

✣

St. Luke 4, 1–13; St. Matthew 4, 1–11

FIRST POINT. After He had been baptized, Jesus went to the desert where He fasted for forty days and forty nights.

SECOND POINT. He was tempted by the enemy three times: "The tempter drew near and said to Him, 'If thou art the Son of God command that these stones become loaves.... Cast thyself down.... All these things I will give thee if falling down thou wilt worship me!'"

THIRD POINT. "The angels came and ministered to Him."

275. THE VOCATION OF THE APOSTLES

FIRST POINT. St. Peter and St. Andrew seem to have been called three times. First, to some knowledge of our Lord. This is evident from the first chapter of St. John. Secondly, to a following of Christ in some way, but with the intention of returning to the possessions they had left. St. Luke tells us this in the fifth chapter. Thirdly, to follow Christ our Lord forever, St. Matthew, chapter four, and St. Mark, chapter one.

SECOND POINT. He called Philip, as we read in the first chapter of St. John. He called Matthew, as is recorded by St. Matthew himself in the ninth chapter.

THIRD POINT. He called the other Apostles, of whom no special call is mentioned in the Gospel.

Three other points must also be considered:

1. That the Apostles were uneducated and from a humble condition of life.

2. The dignity to which they were so gently called.

3. The gifts and graces by which they were raised above all the Fathers of the Old and New Testaments.

276. THE FIRST MIRACLE PERFORMED AT THE MARRIAGE FEAST OF CANA IN GALILEE

✣

St. John 2, 1–11

FIRST POINT. Christ our Lord and the disciples were invited to the marriage feast.

SECOND POINT. His Mother calls attention to the shortage of wine, saying to Him, "They have no wine." She bids the servants, "Whatsoever He shall say to you do."

THIRD POINT. He changed the water into wine, "And he manifested his glory and his disciples believed in him."

277. CHRIST CASTS THE SELLERS FROM THE TEMPLE

✣

St. John 2, 13–22

FIRST POINT. With a whip made of cords He casts all those who sell out of the Temple.

SECOND POINT. He overturned the tables and scattered the money of the wealthy money changers who were in the Temple.

THIRD POINT. To the poor vendors of doves He said kindly, "Take these away! Make not the house of my Father a house of traffic."

278. THE SERMON ON THE MOUNT

✣

St. Matthew 5

FIRST POINT. He proposes the eight beatitudes to His beloved disciples apart: "Blessed are the poor in spirit...the meek...the merciful...they that mourn...they that hunger...the peacemakers...those that suffer persecution."

SECOND POINT. He exhorts them to use their talents, "So let your light shine before men in order that they may see your good works and glorify your Father in heaven."

THIRD POINT. He shows Himself not a transgressor of the Law but a fulfiller. He explains the commandments not to kill, not to commit adultery, not to swear falsely, and commands us to love our enemies: "I say, love your enemies, do good to them that hate you."

279. CHRIST CALMS THE STORM

✣

St. Matthew 8, 23–27

FIRST POINT. While Christ our Lord was asleep in the boat on the sea, a great storm arose.

SECOND POINT. His terrified disciples awaken Him. He reprehends them for the little faith they have, and says to them, "Why are ye afraid, O ye of little faith?"

THIRD POINT. He commanded the wind and sea to cease, and they obeyed, and the sea became calm. And the men marveled, saying, "What manner of man is this that even the winds and the sea obey him?"

280.   CHRIST WALKS UPON THE WATERS

✤

St. Matthew 14, 22–33

FIRST POINT.   While Christ our Lord remained on the mountain, He commanded His disciples to go away in the boat, and after He had dismissed the crowd, He began to pray alone.

SECOND POINT.   The boat was buffeted by the waves. Christ came toward them walking upon the waters, and the disciples thought they saw an apparition.

THIRD POINT.   Christ says to them, "It is I, fear not." St. Peter at His command walked upon the waters and came to Jesus, but when he doubted, he began to sink. Christ saved him and reprehended him for his little faith. They entered into the boat and the wind ceased.

281.   THE APOSTLES ARE SENT TO PREACH

✤

St. Matthew 10, 1–16

FIRST POINT.   Christ calls His beloved disciples and gives them power to cast out devils from the bodies of men, and to heal all their infirmities.

SECOND POINT.   He teaches them prudence and patience, "Behold I send you forth as sheep into midst of wolves. Be ye therefore wise as serpents and guileless as doves."

THIRD POINT.   He tells them how they should go, "Do not possess gold or silver." "Freely ye have received, freely give." And he told them what to preach: "As ye go, preach saying, 'The kingdom of God is at hand.'"

282. THE CONVERSION OF MAGDALENE

✣

St. Luke 7, 36–50

FIRST POINT. Magdalene, carrying an alabaster vase full of ointment, enters the house of the Pharisee where Christ is seated at table.

SECOND POINT. She stood behind our Lord near His feet, and
began to wash them with her tears, and wiped them with her hair.
She kissed His feet, and anointed them with ointment.

THIRD POINT. When the Pharisee accused Magdalene, Christ
spoke in her defense, saying, "Her many sins are forgiven because
she has loved much. . . . But he said to the woman, 'Thy faith hath
saved thee, go in peace.' "

283. CHRIST FEEDS FIVE THOUSAND

✣

St. Matthew 14, 13–21

FIRST POINT. Since it was getting late, the disciples asked Jesus to
dismiss the multitude of people who were with Him.

SECOND POINT. Christ our Lord commanded them to bring the
loaves of bread to Him, and ordered the people to sit down. Then
He blessed the bread, broke it, and gave it to the disciples who gave
it to the multitude.

THIRD POINT. "And they all ate and had their fill, and they took up
the fragments that were left over, twelve full baskets."

284. THE TRANSFIGURATION

✣

St. Matthew 17, 1–9

FIRST POINT. Jesus took with Him His beloved disciples, Peter,
James, and John, and He was transfigured before them. His face
became resplendent as the sun, and His garments like snow.

SECOND POINT.   He spoke with Moses and Elias.

THIRD POINT.   When St. Peter said that they should build three tabernacles, a voice was heard from heaven, saying, "This is my beloved Son. . . . Hear ye him." When the disciples heard this voice, they fell down for fear, their faces to the ground. Jesus came and touched them, and said to them, "Arise and fear not. . . . Tell not the vision to any one till the Son of Man be risen from the dead."

285.   THE RAISING OF LAZARUS
✢
St. John 11, 1–45

FIRST POINT.   Mary and Martha inform Jesus of the sickness of Lazarus. After He was informed of this, He delayed for two days that the miracle might be more evident.

SECOND POINT.   Before He raised him, He asked faith of both Mary and Martha, saying, "I am the resurrection and the life. He that believeth in me even though he die shall live."

THIRD POINT.   Jesus raises him after He had wept and said a prayer. The way in which He raised him was by a command, "Lazarus, come forth."

286.   THE SUPPER AT BETHANY
✢
St. Matthew 26, 6–10

FIRST POINT.   Our Lord eats in the house of Simon the leper together with Lazarus.

SECOND POINT.   Mary pours out the ointment upon the head of Christ.

THIRD POINT.   Judas murmurs the words, "Why this waste?" But Jesus defends Magdalene again, saying, "Why do you trouble this woman? She hath wrought a good work upon me."

287.   PALM SUNDAY

✢

St. Matthew 21, 1–17

FIRST POINT.   Our Lord sends for the ass and the foal, saying, "Loose them and bring them to me, and if anyone say aught to you, you shall say, 'The Lord hath need of them,' and straightway he will let them go."

SECOND POINT.   After the ass was covered with the garments of the Apostles, Jesus mounted it.

THIRD POINT.   The people came forth to meet Jesus, and spread their garments and the branches of trees in the way, saying, "Hosanna to the Son of David! Blessed is he that cometh in the name of the Lord! Hosanna in the highest!"

288.   JESUS PREACHES IN THE TEMPLE

✢

St. Luke 19, 47–48

FIRST POINT.   He was teaching daily in the temple.

SECOND POINT.   After His teaching, since there was no one in Jerusalem who would receive Him, He returned to Bethania.

289.   THE LAST SUPPER

✢

St. Matthew 26, 20–30; St. John 13, 1–30

FIRST POINT.   He eats the Paschal Lamb with His disciples, to whom He predicts His death: "Amen I say to you, one of you shall betray me."

SECOND POINT.   He washes the feet of the disciples, even those of Judas. He begins with St. Peter, but St. Peter, considering the majesty of the Lord and his own lowliness, does not want to permit it, and says, "Lord dost thou wash my feet?" St. Peter did not know that Christ was giving an example of humility in this, and therefore, Jesus said to him, "I have given you an example that as I have done you also ought to do."

Third Point. He institutes the most holy Sacrifice of the Eucharist, the greatest proof of His love. He says to them, "Take and eat." When the supper was finished, Judas went forth to sell our Lord.

290. FROM THE LAST SUPPER TO THE AGONY INCLUSIVE

✣

St. Matthew 26, 30–46; St. Mark 14, 32–44

First Point.   When the Supper was finished, and after the hymn was sung, Jesus, full of fear, goes forth with His disciples to Mt. Olivet. He left eight of them in Gethsemani, saying, "Sit you here whilst I go yonder and pray."

Second Point.   Accompanied by St. Peter, St. James, and St. John, He prays three times to the Father, saying, "My Father, if it be possible let this cup pass from me, yet not as I will but as thou wilt." "And falling into an agony He prayed the more earnestly."

Third Point.   So great was the fear that overwhelmed Him that he said: "My soul is sorrowful unto death." And He sweat blood so copiously that St. Luke says, "His sweat became as drops of blood falling down to the ground." This supposes that His garments were saturated with blood.

291.   FROM THE GARDEN TO THE
HOUSE OF ANNAS INCLUSIVE

✣

*St. Matthew 26, 47–58; St. Luke 22, 47–57; St. Mark
14, 44–54 and 66-68*

FIRST POINT.   Our Lord allows Himself to be kissed by Judas, and to be seized as a robber. He says to them: "Are ye come out as against a robber with swords and clubs to arrest me? Day after day I sat in the temple teaching and you seized me not." When he said, "Whom seek ye?" His enemies fell to the ground.

SECOND POINT.   St. Peter wounds the servant of the High Priest. The meek Lord says to him, "Put back thy sword into its place." And He healed the wound of the servant.

THIRD POINT.   Deserted by His disciples, He is led to Annas. There St. Peter, who had followed Him afar off, denied Him once. Christ was struck in the face and asked, "Answerest thou thus the High Priest?"

292.   FROM THE HOUSE OF ANNAS
TO THE HOUSE OF CAIPHAS INCLUSIVE

✣

St. Matthew 26; St. Mark 14; St. Luke 22; St. John 18

FIRST POINT.   They led Him bound from the house of Annas to that of Caiphas, where St. Peter denied Him twice. When our Lord looked upon him, he went out and wept bitterly.

SECOND POINT.   Jesus remained bound the whole night.

THIRD POINT.   Those who kept Him bound scoffed at Him, buffeted Him, covered His face and struck Him with the palms of their hands, and asked Him, "Prophesy who it was that struck Thee." And similar things they said, blaspheming Him.

293.   FROM THE HOUSE OF CAIPHAS
      TO THE HOUSE OF PILATE INCLUSIVE

✤

St. Matthew 27; St. Luke 23; St. Mark 15

First Point.   The whole multitude of Jews took Him to Pilate, and accused Him before the governor, saying, "We have found this man subverting our nation and forbidding to give tribute to Caesar."

Second Point.   After Pilate had examined Him several times, he said: "I find no crime in this man."

Third Point.   Barabbas, the robber, was preferred to Him: "They, therefore, shouted again, saying, 'Not this man but Barabbas.'"

294.   FROM THE HOUSE OF PILATE
          TO THE HOUSE OF HEROD

✤

St. Luke 23, 6–11

First Point.   Pilate sent Jesus, the Galilean, to Herod, the tetrarch of Galilee.

Second Point.   Herod curiously asked many questions, and Jesus answered nothing, though the scribes and priests accused Him constantly.

Third Point.   Herod and his court mocked Jesus, and clothed Him with a white garment.

295.   FROM THE HOUSE OF HEROD
             TO THAT OF PILATE

✤

St. Matthew 27; St. Luke 23; St. Mark 15; St. John 19

First Point.   Herod sent Jesus back to Pilate, and because of this they became friends, though before they were enemies.

SECOND POINT.   Pilate took Jesus and had Him scourged, and the soldiers made a crown of thorns and placed it upon His head. They put a purple cloak about Him, and came to Him and said, "Hail king of the Jews!" "And they gave Him blows."

THIRD POINT.   Pilate led Him forth before all: "Jesus, therefore, came forth, wearing the crown of thorns, and the purple garment. And he said to them, 'Behold the man!'" When the chief priests saw Him they cried out, "Crucify him, Crucify him!"

296.   FROM THE HOUSE OF PILATE TO THE CROSS INCLUSIVE

✢

St. John 19, 13–22

FIRST POINT.   Sitting in judgment, Pilate delivered up Jesus to be crucified after the Jews had denied that He was their king, saying, "We have no king but Caesar."

SECOND POINT.   He carried the cross upon His shoulders, and when He was no longer able to do so, Simon of Cyrene was forced to carry it after Jesus.

THIRD POINT.   They crucified Him between two thieves. The title placed over the cross read: "Jesus of Nazareth, King of the Jews."

297.   JESUS DIES UPON THE CROSS

✢

St. John 19, 23–37; St. Matthew 27, 35–52; St. Mark 15, 24–38; St. Luke 23, 34–46

FIRST POINT.   He spoke seven words upon the cross: He prayed for those who crucified Him; He pardoned the thief; He recommended St. John to His Mother; He said with a loud voice, "I thirst," and they gave Him vinegar to drink; He said that He was forsaken; He said, "It is consummated"; He said, "Father, into thy hands I commend my spirit."

Second Point. The sun was darkened, the rocks rent, the graves opened, and the veil of the Temple was torn in two from top to bottom.

Third Point. They blasphemed Him, saying, "Thou who wouldst overthrow the temple . . . come down from the cross." His garments were divided, His side was pierced with a lance, and blood and water came forth.

298.   ## FROM THE CROSS TO THE SEPULCHER INCLUSIVE

✤

Ibidem

First Point. He was taken down from the cross by Joseph and Nicodemus in the presence of His sorrowful Mother.

Second Point. The body was borne to the sepulcher, and anointed, and buried.

Third Point. Guards were stationed.

299.   ## THE RESURRECTION OF CHRIST OUR LORD— THE FIRST APPARITION

First Point. He appeared to the Virgin Mary. Though this is not mentioned explicitly in the Scripture it must be considered as stated when Scripture says that He appeared to many others. For Scripture supposes that we have understanding, as it is written, "Are you also without understanding?"

300.   THE SECOND APPARITION

✣

St. Mark 16, 1–11

FIRST POINT.   Very early in the morning Mary Magdalene, Mary the mother of James, and Salome go to the tomb. They say to one another, "Who will roll away the stone for us from the entrance of the tomb?"

SECOND POINT.   They see the stone rolled back and the angel who says to them: "Ye seek Jesus of Nazareth. . . . He is risen, he is not here."

THIRD POINT.   He appeared to Mary who remained near the tomb after the others left.

301.   THE THIRD APPARITION

✣

St. Matthew 28

FIRST POINT.   The two Marys go from the sepulcher with great fear and joy to announce the Resurrection of the Lord to the disciples.

SECOND POINT.   Christ our Lord appears to them on the way, and says to them, "Hail!" and they went up to Him, and fell down at His feet and adored Him.

THIRD POINT.   Jesus says to them: "Fear not! Go tell my brethren to depart into Galilee. There they shall see me."

302.   THE FOURTH APPARITION

✣

St. Luke 24, 9–12 and 33–34

FIRST POINT.   When St. Peter heard from the women that Christ has risen, he went with haste to the tomb.

SECOND POINT. He entered the tomb and saw only the linens with which the body of Christ had been covered, and nothing more.

THIRD POINT. While St. Peter was thinking of these things, Christ appeared to him. That is why the Apostles said, "The Lord is risen indeed and has appeared to Simon."

303.

THE FIFTH APPARITION

✤

St. Luke 24

FIRST POINT. He appeared to His disciples who were going to Emmaus and were talking of Christ.

SECOND POINT. He reprehends them, showing them by the Scriptures that Christ must die and rise again: "O senseless men and slow of heart to believe all that the prophets have spoken! Ought not Christ to have suffered these things and so to enter into His glory?"

THIRD POINT. At their request He remains there, and was with them till He gave them Holy Communion. Then He disappeared. Thereupon they returned to the disciples and told them how they recognized Him in Communion.

304.

THE SIXTH APPARITION

✤

St. John 20, 19–23

FIRST POINT. The disciples, except St. Thomas, were gathered together "for fear of the Jews."

SECOND POINT. Jesus appeared to them, the doors being locked, and standing in their midst said, "Peace be to you!"

THIRD POINT. He gives them the Holy Spirit, saying, "Receive ye the Holy Ghost, whose sins you shall forgive, they are forgiven."

305.   ## THE SEVENTH APPARITION

✣

St. John 20, 24–29

FIRST POINT.   Since St. Thomas was not present at the preceding apparition, he would not believe and said, "Unless I see . . . I will not believe."

SECOND POINT.   Eight days after, Jesus appeared them, the doors closed, and He said to Thomas, "Reach hither thy finger and see . . . and be not unbelieving but believing."

THIRD POINT.   St. Thomas believed, saying, "My Lord and my God." Christ said to him, "Blessed are they who have not seen and have believed."

306.   ## THE EIGHTH APPARITION

✣

St. John 21, 1–17

FIRST POINT.   Jesus appeared to seven of His disciples who were fishing. They had fished all night and caught nothing. But casting the net at His command "they were not able to haul it in for the multitude of fishes."

SECOND POINT.   Through this miracle St. John recognized Him, and said to St. Peter, "It is the Lord." St. Peter cast himself into the sea and came to Christ.

THIRD POINT.   He gave them bread and part of a broiled fish to eat. After He had first tested three times the love of St. Peter, He recommended His sheep to him with the words, "Feed my sheep."

307. THE NINTH APPARITION

St. Matthew 28, 16–20

FIRST POINT. The disciples at the command of Christ go to Mt. Thabor.

SECOND POINT. Christ appears to them and says: "All power is given to me in heaven and on earth."

THIRD POINT. He sent them throughout the world to teach, saying, "Go ye, therefore, make disciples of all nations, baptizing them in the name of the Father and of the Son and of the Holy Ghost."

308. THE TENTH APPARITION

1 Corinthians 15, 6

"After that He appeared to more than five hundred brethren at once."

309. THE ELEVENTH APPARITION

1 Corinthians 15, 7

"After that he appeared to James."

310. THE TWELFTH APPARITION

He appeared to Joseph of Arimathea, as may be piously believed, and as is read in the *Lives of the Saints*.

311.   THE THIRTEENTH APPARITION

✶

1 Corinthians 15, 8

He appeared to St. Paul after His Ascension: "Last of all, as to one born out of due time, He appeared to me."

He appeared also in soul to the Fathers in limbo;

He appeared to them likewise after He had taken them from there and assumed His body again.

He appeared many times to His disciples and conversed with them.

312. THE ASCENSION OF CHRIST OUR LORD

✶

Acts 1, 1–12

First Point.   After He had manifested Himself for forty days to the Apostles, and had given them many proofs, and worked many miracles, and had spoken to them of the Kingdom of God, He commanded them to await in Jerusalem the promise of the Holy Spirit.

Second Point.   He led them to Mt. Olivet "and He was lifted up before their eyes and a cloud received Him out of their sight."

Third Point.   While they were gazing up into heaven, the angels said to them: "Men of Galilee, why stand ye looking up into heaven? This Jesus who hath been taken up from you into heaven will come after the same manner wherein ye have beheld him going up into heaven."

Rules

RULES FOR THE
DISCERNMENT OF SPIRITS

I

*Rules for understanding to some extent the different
movements produced in the soul and for recognizing
those that are good to admit them, and those that are
bad, to reject them. These rules are more suited to the
first week*

314. 1. In the case of those who go from one mortal sin to another,
the enemy is ordinarily accustomed to propose apparent pleasures.
He fills their imagination with sensual delights and gratifications,
the more readily to keep them in their vices and increase the number of their sins.

With such persons the good spirit uses a method which is the
reverse of the above. Making use of the light of reason, he will
rouse the sting of conscience and fill them with remorse.

315. 2. In the case of those who go on earnestly striving to cleanse
their souls from sin and who seek to rise in the service of God our
Lord to greater perfection, the method pursued is the opposite of
that mentioned in the first rule.

Then it is characteristic of the evil spirit to harass with anxiety,
to afflict with sadness, to raise obstacles backed by fallacious reasonings that disturb the soul. Thus he seeks to prevent the soul
from advancing.

It is characteristic of the good spirit, however, to give courage
and strength, consolations, tears, inspirations, and peace. This He
does by making all easy, by removing all obstacles so that the soul
goes forward in doing good.

316. 3. SPIRITUAL CONSOLATION. I call it consolation when an interior movement is aroused in the soul, by which it is inflamed with
love of its Creator and Lord, and as a consequence, can love no
creature on the face of the earth for its own sake, but only in the
Creator of them all. It is likewise consolation when one sheds tears
that move to the love of God, whether it be because of sorrow for

sins, or because of the sufferings of Christ our Lord, or for any other reason that is immediately directed to the praise and service of God. Finally, I call consolation every increase of faith, hope, and love, and all interior joy that invites and attracts to what is heavenly and to the salvation of one's soul by filling it with peace and quiet in its Creator and Lord.

317. 4. SPIRITUAL DESOLATION. I call desolation what is entirely the opposite of what is described in the third rule, as darkness of soul, turmoil of spirit, inclination to what is low and earthly, restlessness rising from many disturbances and temptations which lead to want of faith, want of hope, want of love. The soul is wholly slothful, tepid, sad, and separated, as it were, from its Creator and Lord. For just as consolation is the opposite of desolation, so the thoughts that spring from consolation are the opposite of those that spring from desolation.

318. 5. In time of desolation we should never make any change, but remain firm and constant in the resolution and decision which guided us the day before the desolation, or in the decision to which we adhered in the preceding consolation. For just as in consolation the good spirit guides and counsels us, so in desolation the evil spirit guides and counsels. Following his counsels we can never find the way to a right decision.

319. 6. Though in desolation we must never change our former resolutions, it will be very advantageous to intensify our activity against the desolation. We can insist more upon prayer, upon meditation, and on much examination of ourselves. We can make an effort in a suitable way to do some penance.

320. 7. When one is in desolation, he should be mindful that God has left him to his natural powers to resist the different agitations and temptations of the enemy in order to try him. He can resist with the help of God, which always remains, though he may not clearly perceive it. For though God has taken from him the abundance of fervor and overflowing love and the intensity of His favors, nevertheless, he has sufficient grace for eternal salvation.

321. 8. When one is in desolation, he should strive to persevere in patience. This reacts against the vexations that have overtaken him. Let him consider, too, that consolation will soon return, and in the meantime, he must diligently use the means against desolation which have been given in the sixth rule.

322. 9. The principal reasons why we suffer from desolation are three:

The first is because we have been tepid and slothful or negligent in our exercises of piety, and so through our own fault spiritual consolation has been taken away from us.

The second reason is because God wishes to try us, to see how much we are worth, and how much we will advance in His service and praise when left without the generous reward of consolations and signal favors.

The third reason is because God wishes to give us a true knowledge and understanding of ourselves, so that we may have an intimate perception of the fact that it is not within our power to acquire and attain great devotion, intense love, tears, or any other spiritual consolation; but that all this is the gift and grace of God our Lord. God does not wish us to build on the property of another, to rise up in spirit in a certain pride and vainglory and attribute to ourselves the devotion and other effects of spiritual consolation.

323. 10. When one enjoys consolation, let him consider how he will conduct himself during the time of ensuing desolation, and store up a supply of strength as defense against that day.

324. 11. He who enjoys consolation should take care to humble himself and lower himself as much as possible. Let him recall how little he is able to do in time of desolation, when he is left without such grace or consolation.

On the other hand, one who suffers desolation should remember that by making use of the sufficient grace offered him, he can do much to withstand all his enemies. Let him find his strength in his Creator and Lord.

325. 12. The enemy conducts himself as a woman. He is a weakling before a show of strength, and a tyrant if he has his will. It is

characteristic of a woman in a quarrel with a man to lose courage and take to flight if the man shows that he is determined and fearless. However, if the man loses courage and begins to flee, the anger, vindictiveness, and rage of the woman surge up and know no bounds. In the same way, the enemy becomes weak, loses courage, and turns to flight with his seductions as soon as one leading a spiritual life faces his temptations boldly, and does exactly the opposite of what he suggests. However, if one begins to be afraid and to lose courage in temptations, no wild animal on earth can be more fierce than the enemy of our human nature. He will carry out his perverse intentions with consummate malice.

326. 13. Our enemy may also be compared in his manner of acting to a false lover. He seeks to remain hidden and does not want to be discovered. If such a lover speaks with evil intention to the daughter of a good father, or to the wife of a good husband, and seeks to seduce them, he wants his words and solicitations kept secret. He is greatly displeased if his evil suggestions and depraved intentions are revealed by the daughter to her father, or by the wife to her husband. Then he readily sees he will not succeed in what he has begun. In the same way, when the enemy of our human nature tempts a just soul with his wiles and seductions, he earnestly desires that they be received secretly and kept secret. But if one manifests them to a confessor, or to some other spiritual person who understands his deceits and malicious designs, the evil one is very much vexed. For he knows that he cannot succeed in his evil undertaking, once his evident deceits have been revealed.

327. 14. The conduct of our enemy may also be compared to the tactics of a leader intent upon seizing and plundering a position he desires. A commander and leader of an army will encamp, explore the fortifications and defenses of the stronghold, and attack at the weakest point. In the same way, the enemy of our human nature investigates from every side all our virtues, theological, cardinal, and moral. Where he finds the defenses of eternal salvation weakest and most deficient, there he attacks and tries to take us by storm.

328. RULES FOR DISCERNMENT OF SPIRITS

II

Further rules for understanding the different movements
produced in the soul. They serve for a more accurate
discernment of spirits and are more suitable for the
second week

329. 1. It is characteristic of God and His Angels, when they act upon the soul, to give true happiness and spiritual joy, and to banish all the sadness and disturbances which are caused by the enemy.

It is characteristic of the evil one to fight against such happiness and consolation by proposing fallacious reasonings, subtleties, and continual deceptions.

330. 2. God alone can give consolation to the soul without any previous cause. It belongs solely to the Creator to come into a soul, to leave it, to act upon it, to draw it wholly to the love of His Divine Majesty. I said without previous cause, that is, without any preceding perception or knowledge of any subject by which a soul might be led to such a consolation through its own acts of intellect and will.

331. 3. If a cause precedes, both the good angel and the evil spirit can give consolation to a soul, but for a quite different purpose. The good angel consoles for the progress of the soul, that it may advance and rise to what is more perfect. The evil spirit consoles for purposes that are the contrary, and that afterwards he might draw the soul to his own perverse intentions and wickedness.

332. 4. It is a mark of the evil spirit to assume the appearance of an angel of light. He begins by suggesting thoughts that are suited to a devout soul, and ends by suggesting his own. For example, he will suggest holy and pious thoughts that are wholly in conformity with the sanctity of the soul. Afterwards, he will endeavor little by little to end by drawing the soul into his hidden snares and evil designs.

333. 5. We must carefully observe the whole course of our thoughts. If the beginning and middle and end of the course of thoughts are wholly good and directed to what is entirely right, it is

a sign that they are from the good angel. But the course of thoughts suggested to us may terminate in something evil, or distracting, or less good than the soul had formerly proposed to do. Again, it may end in what weakens the soul, or disquiets it; or by destroying the peace, tranquillity, and quiet which it had before, it may cause disturbance to the soul. These things are a clear sign that the thoughts are proceeding from the evil spirit, the enemy of our progress and eternal salvation.

334. 6. When the enemy of our human nature has been detected and recognized by the trail of evil marking his course and by the wicked end to which he leads us, it will be profitable for one who has been tempted to review immediately the whole course of the temptation. Let him consider the series of good thoughts, how they arose, how the evil one gradually attempted to make him step down from the state of spiritual delight and joy in which he was, till finally he drew him to his wicked designs. The purpose of this review is that once such an experience has been understood and carefully observed, we may guard ourselves for the future against the customary deceits of the enemy.

335. 7. In souls that are progressing to greater perfection, the action of the good angel is delicate, gentle, delightful. It may be compared to a drop of water penetrating a sponge.

The action of the evil spirit upon such souls is violent, noisy, and disturbing. It may be compared to a drop of water falling upon a stone.

In souls that are going from bad to worse, the action of the spirits mentioned above is just the reverse. The reason for this is to be sought in the opposition or similarity of these souls to the different kinds of spirits. When the disposition is contrary to that of the spirits, they enter with noise and commotion that are easily perceived. When the disposition is similar to that of the spirits, they enter silently, as one coming into his own house when the doors are open.

336. 8. When consolation is without previous cause, as was said, there can be no deception in it, since it can proceed from God our Lord only. But a spiritual person who has received such a consolation must consider it very attentively, and must cautiously distin-

guish the actual time of the consolation from the period which follows it. At such a time the soul is still fervent and favored with the grace and aftereffects of the consolation which has passed. In this second period the soul frequently forms various resolutions and plans which are not granted directly by God our Lord. They may come from our own reasoning on the relations of our concepts and on the consequences of our judgments, or they may come from the good or evil spirit. Hence, they must be carefully examined before they are given full approval and put into execution.

337.

RULES FOR THE DISTRIBUTION OF ALMS

✣

In the ministry of distributing alms the following rules should be observed

338. 1. If I distribute alms to my relatives or friends or persons to whom I am attached, there are four things that must be considered. Some of these were mentioned in treating the Choice of a Way of Life.

The first is that the love that moves me and causes me to give the alms must be from above, that is, from the love of God our Lord. Hence, I should be conscious within myself that God is the motive of the greater or less love that I bear toward these persons, and that God is manifestly the cause of my loving them more.

339. 2. I should place before my mind a person whom I have never seen or known, and whom I wish to be wholly perfect in the office and state of life which he occupies. Now the same standard of action that I would like him to follow in his way of distributing alms for the greater glory of God and the perfection of his soul I myself will observe, and do neither more nor less. The same rule I would like him to follow, and the norm I judge would be for the glory of God I shall abide by myself.

340. 3. I should picture myself at the hour of my death, and ponder well the way and norm I would then wish to have observed in

carrying out the duties of my office. I will lay down the same rule for myself now, and keep it in my distribution of alms.

341. 4. I should imagine myself before my judge on the last day, and weigh well the manner in which I would wish then to have done my duty in carrying out this office. The same rule that I would then wish to have observed I will keep now.

342. 5. When one finds that he is inclined or attached to some persons to whom he wishes to give alms, let him stop and ponder well the four rules given above. He must investigate and test his affection by them. He should not give the alms until in conformity with these rules he has completely put off and cast aside his inordinate attachment.

343. 6. It is true that there is no wrong in receiving the goods of God our Lord for distribution if a person is called by God our Lord to such a service. Nevertheless, there may be question of a fault and excess in the amount he retains and applies to his own needs of what he holds to give to others. Hence one can reform his way of living in his state by the rules given above.

344. 7. For these and many other reasons it will always be better and safer in all matters concerning himself and his household, if one is saving and cuts down expenses as much as possible, if he imitates as closely as he can our great High Priest, model, and guide, Christ our Lord.

It was in conformity with this doctrine that the Third Council of Carthage, at which St. Augustine was present, decided and decreed that the furniture of the bishop should be cheap and poor.

The same consideration applies to all stations in life, but attention must be given to adapting it to each one's condition and rank.

In matrimony we have the example of St. Joachim and St. Anne. They divided their resources into three parts. The first they gave to the poor. The second they donated to the ministrations and services of the Temple. The third they used for the support of themselves and their household.

345.
SOME NOTES
CONCERNING SCRUPLES

✳

*The following notes will aid us to understand scruples
and the temptations of our enemy*

346. 1. It is common for people to speak of something as a scruple though it has proceeded from their own judgment and free will, for example, when I freely decide that something is a sin which is not a sin. Thus it may happen that after one has chanced to step upon a cross formed by straws, he decides according to his own way of thinking that he has sinned. In reality, this is an erroneous judgment and not a real scruple.

347. 2. After I have stepped upon such a cross, or after anything else I may have thought, said, or done, the suggestion may come to me from without that I have sinned, and on the other hand, it may seem to me that I have not sinned. Then if I continue to be anxious about the matter, doubting and not doubting that I sinned, there is a real scruple properly so called and a temptation from our enemy.

348. 3. The kind of scruple mentioned in the first note should be much abhorred, since it is wholly erroneous. But the scruple described in the second note may for a while prove to be of no little advantage for a soul devoting itself to the spiritual life. It may in fact greatly purify and cleanse such a soul by doing much to free it from even the appearance of sin. St. Gregory has said: "It is characteristic of a devout soul to see a fault where there is none."

349. 4. The enemy considers carefully whether one has a lax or a delicate conscience. If one has a delicate conscience, the evil one seeks to make it excessively sensitive, in order to disturb and upset it more easily. Thus, if he sees that one will not consent to mortal sin, or venial sin, or even to the appearance of deliberate sin, since he cannot cause him to fall in a matter that appears sinful, he strives to make the soul judge that there is a sin, for example, in a word or passing thought where there is no sin.

If one has a lax conscience, the enemy endeavors to make it more so. Thus, if before a soul did not bother about venial sin, the enemy will contrive that it make light of mortal sin. If before it paid some heed to venial sin, his efforts will be that now it cares much less or not at all.

350. 5. A soul that wishes to make progress in the spiritual life must always act in a manner contrary to that of the enemy. If the enemy seeks to make the conscience lax, one must endeavor to make it more sensitive. If the enemy strives to make the conscience delicate with a view to leading it to excess, the soul must endeavor to establish itself firmly in a moderate course so that in all things it may preserve itself in peace.

351. 6. If a devout soul wishes to do something that is not contrary to the spirit of the Church or the mind of superiors and that may be for the glory of God our Lord, there may come a thought or temptation from without not to say or do it. Apparent reasons may be adduced for this, such as that it is motivated by vainglory or some other imperfect intention, etc. In such cases one should raise his mind to his Creator and Lord, and if he sees that what he is about to do is in keeping with God's service, or at least not opposed to it, he should act directly against the temptation. According to St. Bernard, we must answer the tempter, "I did not undertake this because of you, and I am not going to relinquish it because of you."

352.   RULES FOR THINKING
WITH THE CHURCH

✣

*The following rules should be observed to foster the true
attitude of mind we ought to have in the church
militant*

353. 1. We must put aside all judgment of our own, and keep the mind ever ready and prompt to obey in all things the true Spouse of Christ our Lord, our holy Mother, the hierarchical Church.

354. 2. We should praise sacramental confession, the yearly reception of the Most Blessed Sacrament, and praise more highly

monthly reception, and still more weekly Communion, provided requisite and proper dispositions are present.

355. 3. We ought to praise the frequent hearing of Mass, the singing of hymns, psalmody, and long prayers whether in the church or outside; likewise, the hours arranged at fixed times for the whole Divine Office, for every kind of prayer, and for the canonical hours.

356. 4. We must praise highly religious life, virginity, and continency; and matrimony ought not be praised as much as any of these.

357. 5. We should praise vows of religion, obedience, poverty, chastity, and vows to perform other works of supererogation conducive to perfection. However, it must be remembered that a vow deals with matters that lead us closer to evangelical perfection. Hence, whatever tends to withdraw one from perfection may not be made the object of a vow, for example, a business career, the married state, and so forth.

358. 6. We should show our esteem for the relics of the saints by venerating them and praying to the saints. We should praise visits to the Station Churches, pilgrimages, indulgences, jubilees, crusade indults, and the lighting of candles in churches.

359. 7. We must praise the regulations of the Church with regard to fast and abstinence, for example, in Lent, on Ember Days, Vigils, Fridays, and Saturdays. We should praise works of penance, not only those that are interior but also those that are exterior.

360. 8. We ought to praise not only the building and adornment of churches, but also images and veneration of them according to the subject they represent.

361. 9. Finally, we must praise all the commandments of the Church, and be on the alert to find reasons to defend them, and by no means in order to criticize them.

362. 10. We should be more ready to approve and praise the orders, recommendations, and way of acting of our superiors than to find fault with them. Though some of the orders, etc., may not

have been praiseworthy, yet to speak against them, either when preaching in public or in speaking before the people, would rather be the cause of murmuring and scandal than of profit. As a consequence, the people would become angry with their superiors, whether secular or spiritual. But while it does harm in the absence of our superiors to speak evil of them before the people, it may be profitable to discuss their bad conduct with those who can apply a remedy.

363. 11. We should praise both positive theology and that of the Scholastics.

It is characteristic of the positive doctors, such as St. Augustine, St. Jerome, St. Gregory, and others, to rouse the affections so that we are moved to love and serve God our Lord in all things.

On the other hand, it is more characteristic of the scholastic doctors, such as St. Thomas, St. Bonaventure, the Master of the Sentences, and others, to define and state clearly, according to the needs of our times, the doctrines that are necessary for eternal salvation, and that more efficaciously help to refute all errors and expose all fallacies.

Further, just because scholastic doctors belong to more recent times, they not only have the advantage of correct understanding of Holy Scripture and of the teaching of the saints and positive doctors, but, enlightened by the grace of God, they also make use of the decisions of the Councils and of the definitions and decrees of our Holy Mother Church.

364. 12. We must be on our guard against making comparisons between those who are still living and the saints who have gone before us, for no small error is committed if we say: "This man is wiser than St. Augustine," "He is another St. Francis or even greater," "He is equal to St. Paul in goodness and sanctity," and so on.

365. 13. If we wish to proceed securely in all things, we must hold fast to the following principle: What seems to me white, I will believe black if the hierarchical Church so defines. For I must be convinced that in Christ our Lord, the bridegroom, and in His spouse the Church, only one Spirit holds sway, which governs and rules for the salvation of souls. For it is by the same Spirit and Lord

who gave the Ten Commandments that our Holy Mother Church is ruled and governed.

366. 14. Granted that it be very true that no one can be saved without being predestined and without having faith and grace, still we must be very cautious about the way in which we speak of all these things and discuss them with others.

367. 15. We should not make it a habit of speaking much of predestination. If somehow at times it comes to be spoken of, it must be done in such a way that the people are not led into any error. They are at times misled, so that they say: "Whether I shall be saved or lost, has already been determined, and this cannot be changed whether my actions are good or bad." So they become indolent and neglect the works that are conducive to the salvation and spiritual progress of their souls.

368. 16. In the same way, much caution is necessary, lest by much talk about faith, and much insistence on it without any distinctions or explanations, occasion be given to the people, whether before or after they have faith informed by charity, to become slothful and lazy in good works.

369. 17. Likewise we ought not to speak of grace at such length and with such emphasis that the poison of doing away with liberty is engendered.

Hence, as far as is possible with the help of God, one may speak of faith and grace that the Divine Majesty may be praised. But let it not be done in such a way, above all not in times which are as dangerous as ours, that works and free will suffer harm, or that they are considered of no value.

370. 18. Though the zealous service of God our Lord out of pure love should be esteemed above all, we ought also to praise highly the fear of the Divine Majesty. For not only filial fear but also servile fear is pious and very holy. When nothing higher or more useful is attained, it is very helpful for rising from mortal sin, and once this is accomplished, one may easily advance to filial fear, which is wholly pleasing and agreeable to God our Lord since it is inseparably associated with the love of Him.

NOTES

PREFACE BY AVERY DULLES, S.J.

1. Cándido de Dalmases, "Introducción" to *The Spiritual Exercises* in Ignacio Iparraguirre and others, *San Ignacio de Loyola, Obras: Edición Manual* (Madrid: Biblioteca de Autores Cristianos, 1991), pp. 181–209, at 181.
2. See the translator's note on section 169.
3. The French semiologist Roland Barthes distinguishes four "texts" or levels of meaning in *The Exercises*. The "literal" meaning, he holds, is addressed by Ignatius to the director. The "semantic" text is addressed by the director to the exercitant on the basis of the literal text. The third text, the "allegorical," is addressed by the exercitant to God, and the final text, the "anagogic," is addressed by God to the exercitant. The contemporary reader must take account of all these senses. See Roland Barthes, *Sade/Fourier/Loyola* (New York: Hill and Wang, 1976), pp. 38–75, esp. pp. 41–48.
4. Pelagianism, named for the British monk Pelagius (d. ca. 420), is the theological system that holds that human beings take the initial and fundamental steps toward salvation by their own initiative without the need of divine grace. The system was opposed by Augustine and condemned by a series of Church councils.
5. Ignatian obedience does not involve a total suppression of one's personal judgment. The subject has the responsibility of judging that the action commanded is not sinful and is entitled to "represent" to the superior any reasons that seem to indicate that the order is unwise. Such representation is, however, to be done with humility and with a willingness to submit to the superior's judgment if it remains unchanged. In general, one

should avoid publicly contesting the judgment or denouncing the conduct of superiors (sections 361–62).

6. The prayer "Soul of Christ," printed at the beginning of many modern versions of *The Spiritual Exercises,* was not part of the original text. Editors in later centuries, finding that their readers no longer knew the prayer by heart, decided to print it for their benefit.

7. I have illustrated this indebtedness in the cases of Teilhard de Chardin, de Lubac, Rahner, and Balthasar in my article "The Ignatian Charism and Contemporary Theology," *America* 176 (April 26, 1997), pp. 14–22. Rahner holds that *The Spiritual Exercises,* as an original and creative assimilation of God's revelation in Christ, has something to say to theology that theology could not otherwise come to know. It can therefore serve as a source and subject of tomorrow's theology. See Karl Rahner, *The Dynamic Element in the Church* (New York: Herder and Herder, 1964), pp. 86–87.

TRANSLATOR'S PREFACE

1. *Monumenta Historica Societatis Jesu, Monumenta Ignatiana, Series Secunda. Exercitia Spiritualia,* Madrid, 1919.

2. There are three common translations of the text: Morris, John, *Text of the Spiritual Exercises of St. Ignatius,* Westminster, Md., 1934; Mullen, Elder, *The Spiritual Exercises of St. Ignatius,* New York, 1914; Benedictines of Stanbrook, *The Spiritual Exercises of St. Ignatius Literally Translated,* London, 1928. There are three common translations with commentary: Rickaby, Joseph, *The Spiritual Exercises, Spanish and English,* London, 1915; Longridge, M. H., *The Spiritual Exercises of St. Ignatius Loyola,* London, 1919; Ambruzzi, Aloysius, *The Spiritual Exercises of St. Ignatius,* Mangalore, 1931.

3. *Des Heiligen Ignatius von Loyola Geistlichen Uebungen nach dem Spanischen Urtext Uebertragen, 2 Aufl.,* Regensburg, 1922.

4. Calveras, José, S.J., *Ejercicios Espirituales, Directorio y Documentos,* Barcelona, 1944.

5. *Ars Ignatiana, Barcelona,* 1888; *Los Ejercicios en si Mismos y en su Aplicación,* Manresa, 1896; *Estudio Sobre el Texto,* Manresa, 1916.

Notes on the Translation

The purpose of these notes is to give the reasons for the translation adopted when it differs from the traditional wording.

The marginal number will be placed over the comment on any word or passage occurring in that section. But first a note on the prayer "Soul of Christ."

Soul of Christ

In the breviary and in the missal this prayer occurs in the Thanksgiving after Mass under the heading *Aspirationes Sancti Ignatii.* This is true, of course, not in the sense that St. Ignatius composed the prayer, but in the sense that it was frequently used and recommended by him. It was not prefixed to the Autograph copy or to the early Latin versions. It first appeared at the beginning of the Exercises in an edition printed in Vilna in 1583. Since then it has become the universal custom to place it at the beginning of all copies of the Exercises.

It is referred to in the Exercises where the Triple Colloquy is explained. Here it serves as the vocal prayer at the close of the Second Colloquy. Cf nos. 63, 148. It is also referred to in the Second and Third Methods of Prayer, where it seems to be taken for granted that it is one of the ordinary daily prayers. Cf nos. 253, 258.

1

"Introductory Observations," Spanish, *annotaciones.* Certainly, nothing was further from the mind of St. Ignatius, with his meager education and his limping Spanish, than to invent new words or new meanings for old words. Nor do the ideas contained in the Exercises demand it. It is true that in the Exercises new meanings are given to old words, and new word forms are used. This is due to lack of literary training and lack of knowledge of Castilian. There is no reason to perpetuate these defects. What St. Ignatius meant by *annotaciones* is clear from examining them. They are a numbered series of observations on the Exercises. That they are to serve as some kind of introduction is clearly stated in the title. Evidently, therefore, they are introductory observations, and that is what we have called them. *Annotation* has not such a meaning in current English and apparently never did have.

"**Every method . . . every way,**" in Spanish, *todo modo.* The Spanish seems to be equivalent to, *this whole system.* Cf. Nonell, *Ars Ignatiana,* p. 27. But due to the comparison with bodily exercises it is practically impossible to use any way of expressing this meaning. I have retained the traditional translation which in the context comes practically to the same thing.

"**Taking a walk, journeying on foot, running,**" *pasear, caminar, correr.* An attempt has been made to bring out the shades of meaning. Cf. Nonell, *Estudio sobre el Texto,* Introduction and p. 190, under *caminar.*

"**Attachments,**" Spanish, *affecciones.* St. Ignatius constantly uses *affección* for *afición,* attachment. Both Nonell in *Los Ejercicios en sí Mismos,* p. 14, and the *Monumenta Historica, Exercitia Spiritualia,* p. 127, call attention to this peculiarity. Attachment has commonly been substituted except where it refers to a person.

2

"**Let him adhere to the points,**" *Discuriendo solamente por los puntos.* This translation brings out the position of the adverb. A similar way of rendering this passage was adopted by Feder in German. Cf. also Calveras, *Ejercicios Espirituales, ad loc.,* who shows that the passage was thus understood by Faber and in the old Literal Version, which is probably from the hand of St. Ignatius himself.

"**Better understood,**" *Más . . . sentir.* The Spanish verb *sentir* and the corresponding noun, *sentimiento,* are very frequently used in the transferred sense, *to know, to understand, knowledge, understanding.* The context constantly demands, *perceive, know, understand.*

4

"In our search for the fruit that is proper to the matter assigned," *buscando las cosas según la subiecta materia.* Since *buscar* immediately above refers to searching for the fruits of the exercise, I have retained this meaning here. The German of Feder seems to refer it to the adjustment of the lengths of the Weeks. He also translates *subiecta materia* as *circumstances,* which does not seem good here though in other cases it is the meaning of the term. Cf. Roothaan, note four, on the *Primus modus orandi.* The translation adopted here is also suggested by Calveras, *op. cit., ad loc.*

6

"Additional Directions," *Addiciones.* Cf. note on no. 73.

"Nos. 316–324," all cross references are made in these notes and in the translation by means of the marginal numbers.

14

"Unstable in character," *de ligera condición.* Cf. Calveras, *op. cit., ad loc.*

"Endowments," *subiecto.* I have followed Roothaan's interpretation of *subiecto* as meaning *general ability,* physical and moral. Cf. Roothaan, *ad loc.*; also Calveras, *op. cit., ad loc.* Hence, where this word occurs as referring to a human being, general words are used which do not explicitly specify mental or physical ability, as *fitness, endowments, ability.* Cf. notes on nos. 15, 18. Nonell interprets it as referring to *physical condition* only, cf. *Estudio,* p. 203. This is the interpretation preferred by Feder.

15

"Have the required fitness," *tengan subiecto.* Cf. note above on no. 14.

"Inflame it with love," *Abrasándola.* I have followed the reading of the later Spanish texts. *Abrazándola* seems to be a copyist's error. Cf. Roothaan, *ad loc.*

16

"Inordinately attached," *affectada . . . desordinadamente.* Cf. note on no. 1, referring to *attachment.* Cf. Nonell, *Estudio,* p. 188, on the meanings of the verb *affectar* in the Exercises. Forms of this same verb and of the noun *affección* occur several times in this Observation. If the faulty translation *affection* is retained, it is very confusing.

18

"Of little physical strength," *de poco complisión.* Cf. note of the editor of the Spanish-Latin edition to Father Roothaan's translation. Toward the end of this same Observation the same idea is expressed in Spanish by *de poca capacidad natural.* The two expressions are given the same meaning by Nonell and by Roothaan.

"Has little aptitude," *de poco subiecto.* Cf. notes on nos. 14, 15. Here the meaning is practically equivalent to the English, "He would make a poor subject for the Exercises."

"Choice of a Way of Life," *elección.* Cf. notes on this in no. 169ff.

"Some of the easier exercises," *algunos destos exercicios leves.* Cf. the discussion in Nonell in *Ars Ignatiana* on the meaning of *Exercicios leves.*

20

"Ordinarily," *por via ordinada.* Cf. *Monumenta Historica, op. cit.,* p. 246, note a, the editor thinks that the Spanish text is a copyist's error for *por via ordinaria.*

"United with," *se allega.* For this translation, cf. Calveras, *op. cit., ad loc.*

21

"That no decision is made," *sin determinarse.* Cf. the discussion on the meaning of the verb *determinar* and the noun *determinación* in the Exercises, Nonell, *Estudio,* p. 195. He shows that they mean *decide, choose, decision, choice,* and practically never, *determine, determination.*

22

"Presupposition." This heading in the Autograph occurs only along the top of the page. It has become the custom in later editions to place it over the section.

"Defend the proposition from error," *se salve.* Cf. editor's note to Father Roothaan's translation on this point in the Spanish-Latin edition defending the passive sense of *se salve* instead of the reflexive, *save himself,* which refers to the neighbor and not to the proposition. The translation, *defend the proposition,* makes it very clear that there is no question of the salvation of the soul.

23

"First Principle." The word *first* has been added because the English word *principle* has lost much of the force of the Latin *principium.* Father Morris, though quite literal in his translation, felt the necessity of adding it. Father Feder in German has an equivalent.

"Indifferent." I should like to get rid of this word because of the ambiguous meaning in English, but it is too deeply rooted in spiritual literature, especially that of the Exercises. Further, *detached,* the correct word, presents difficulties in the context.

"Our one desire and choice," *solamente deseando y eligiendo.* Cf. Calveras, *op. cit.,* p. 25, note. He calls attention to the fact that the contemporaries of St. Ignatius, who certainly understood the Spanish of the time, translated in this way.

24

"First Week." This is added before no. 24 for clearness and convenience. Indications of the Weeks occur in the Autograph only as titles along the top of the page. I have placed it here because the Foundation belongs in a sense to all the Weeks.

"Daily Particular Examination," *examen particular y cotidiano.* The modifiers *daily* and *particular* have been changed in position be̶c̶a̶u̶s̶e̶ ̶p̶a̶r̶t̶i̶cular examination has come to be looked upon as one ̶r̶i̶.̶ ̶.̶.̶n̶c̶e, the *and* can be omitted, and could also be omitted because of the difference in idiom in connecting two modifiers of the same word.

27

"Additional Directions," for explanation of this term see note on no. 73.

28

"To which G is prefixed." We are not certain why St. Ignatius used the letter *G.* The editor of the volume on the Exercises in the *Monumenta Historica* thinks it is an abbreviation for the subject of the Particular Examination, for example, *gula.* Roothaan changed it to *D* for day. Cf. *Monumenta Historica, op. cit.,* p. 258.

31

"Note." Throughout the translation this term has been kept, though it does not stand for what we commonly mean by *note* in English. Usually notes are some further explanation of a detail that does not belong in the text, or a reference. In the Exercises they belong to the body of the text and are some additional direction about the Exercises of the Week or of a group of Exercises, or merely a further detail about a previous direction.

They are indicated on the margin in the Autograph. Here they have been centered to draw attention to them and make them easier to find. They are often less prominent in the versions than in the Autograph, which does not make for clearness.

When there is a series of notes in the Autograph, we have merely *note* on the margin and a number. In the translations *NOTES* is placed in the center over the series.

The ways of representing the figure for recording the Particular Examination of Conscience differ in the Autograph and in the Vulgate Version. In the Autograph the lines extend the width of the page, but each succeeding day they come closer together. In the Vulgate they are shortened each day.

33

"Thus overcome," *queda vencido.* The idiomatic use of *quedar* as here, and of *ir,* as in the next section, as auxiliaries of the passive, with little difference of meaning from the ordinary way of expressing the passive, is very common and cannot be imitated in English. In this section we have *queda vencido* for the same idea in no. 34 expressed by *va vencido.* Cf. note in the Spanish-Latin edition to Roothaan's translation, *victa manet.* We have translated actively, *thus overcome,* to keep the subjects the same.

38

The parts in parentheses here and elsewhere are found in the Vulgate Version. I have added such parts because of the great authority of this version, which was made in the lifetime of St. Ignatius, and approved by the Holy See. It was accepted as the official Latin version by the Fifth General Congregation.

47

"A mental representation of the place," *composición viendo el lugar.* The explanation given immediately after these words shows what St. Ignatius meant by them. Evidently the Spanish word *composición* meant something that our English *composition* does not mean. The force of the Latin root must have been strong in his mind. In the second lesson of the breviary for Easter Monday we have a suggestion of what this was. St. Gregory says: *"Fingere namque componere dicimus unde compositores luti figulos vocamus."* Since the English word *composition* has lost this meaning, it is impossible to use it as a translation. Further, in the traditional rendition, "a composition seeing the place," the Spanish *viendo* is not expressed correctly. It should at least be *by seeing.* Evidently the phrase means, "A representation of the place by seeing it in imagination." It has been shortened in the translation to, "A mental representation of the place." "Mental" sufficiently renders "by seeing in imagination."

"Where the object is . . . where Jesus or His Mother is," *donde se halla.* The idiomatic uses of the verb *to find,* so common in some European languages, are almost wholly wanting in English. Hence, we cannot translate, as is often done, "Where he finds himself." The idiomatic uses of the Spanish *hallarse* are constantly recurring. It is an error to translate by *find.* It simply means *to be.*

"See in imagination . . . and consider," *ver con la vista imaginativa y considerar.* Cf. Calveras, *op. cit.,* p. 29, on the "binary character" of the style of St. Ignatius, and the manner of translating. In several places in the translation, if one word expresses the idea sufficiently, the other is omitted.

49

"Note." Failure to emphasize the parts clearly has done much to add to the difficulty of understanding and using the Exercises. The Autograph has more clear indications of this kind than some of the translations. The word *note* has been prominently placed as a heading in this translation. In a few cases where the Autograph omits it, it has been inserted and attention called to it.

50

"That they were," *cómo siendo.* Though the use of *how* after verbs of seeing, considering, and the like is perfectly correct and idiomatic English (Cf. *Webster's New International Dictionary*), it has been replaced very frequently by *that,* which is more common and gives a more even if less graphic translation. *Cómo, how,* is exceedingly common in the language of the Exercises, far more so than is customary in English.

53

"Begin to speak with Him," *hacer un coloquio. Hacer, to make, to do,* is exceedingly common in the Spanish of St. Ignatius. He makes exercises, makes colloquies, makes meditations, makes contemplations, etc. There are very few cases where it is idiomatically correct to keep the verb in English. Hence, we must constantly be looking for another form of expression. Except in very few cases, it has been avoided in the translation. This has caused much apparent change, though it is merely trying to express the ideas in English.

"Reflect on myself," *mirando a mi mismo.* The verb *mirar* is very frequently used in the Exercises in derived meanings, to consider, reflect, examine.

54

"Note on Colloquies." This heading has been added. This is one of the few cases where a note is given which is not clearly indicated in the Autograph. The heading will help both to remember it and to locate it.

55

"Meditation on our sins," *meditación de los pecados.* The article has been changed to a personal pronoun here and in many places in the translation in accordance with the difference of idiom in Spanish and English. We use the personal pronouns very much more.

"Growing and intense sorrow," *crescido y intenso dolor.* The Spanish *crescido,* translated by *growing,* as Father Roothaan points out, means *increasing till it has become great.* It is frequently used by St. Ignatius. Cf. notes on nos. 60 and 320.

56

"The record of my sins," *proceso de los pecados.* The Spanish *proceso* is a legal term, and means both the trial at law and the record of the case. The second meaning is the one that fits here.

Here again the article has been rendered by the possessive. At the close of this section, St. Ignatius makes the construction personal with *I* as subject. The method of translating commented on in the next note gives additional reason for turning the article to the possessive.

"I will call to mind," *traer a la memoria.* St. Ignatius frequently uses an impersonal construction which he turns later to a personal one by the use of the personal pronoun. He begins, "the first point is to see," or even, "the first point, to see," or simply, "to see." Since he often continues with personal pronouns, the whole construction has often been made personal, for example, "First Point. I will see." The emphatic *will* has been preferred to the mere future. At times the imperative has been substituted as circumstances suggested.

58

"Source of contagion and corruption," *una llaga y postema.* Literally, a sore and ulcer. The figure has been changed. The expression adopted seems sufficient to express the idea.

60

"With surging emotion," *con crescido afecto. Surging* is one of the ways by which the adjective *crescido* is translated. Cf. note on no. 55.

61

"Pour out your thoughts," *razonar.* Cf. note in the Spanish-Latin text to no. 199. Roothaan translates by *ratiocinari,* which refers entirely to a reasoning process, for which St. Ignatius uses *raciocinar* and not *razonar.* Nonell, *Estudio,* p. 200, emphasizes the conversational connotation of the verb, and would prefer *converse with.* The note of the editor of the Spanish-Latin text referred to above prefers both, *converse* and *reason.* The translation has been an attempt to join these two. In other places, other ways of doing this have been adopted according to what seemed best under the circumstances.

62

"**With three colloquies,**" *haciendo tres coloquios.* The prepositional phrase has been employed to avoid the unidiomatic *make a colloquy.* Such devices have been continually used, and will not be mentioned hereafter.

71

"**Enter into conversation,**" *haciendo un coloquio.* The translation expresses at once the idea of colloquy and avoids the unidiomatic *make a colloquy.*

"**(Other Exercises).**" The heading and the following note in parentheses have been added in the text. They form a part, we may say, of the approved edition of the Exercises. The two oldest versions, the Vulgate and the Literal Version, contain the note. Both were presented to the Holy See and approved. The Literal Version was probably translated by St. Ignatius himself. We have authority for the statement that he himself added the note. Cf. *Monumenta Historica, op. cit.,* p. 576. There seems to be no reason for adhering to the Autograph in such a way as to assume that it expresses the last word of the author. Wherever a passage in the Vulgate or in the Literal Version seems to be better or to have greater authority it has been used throughout this translation. As a matter of fact, the Vulgate, which was published in the lifetime of St. Ignatius, and carefully corrected and approved by the Fifth General Congregation, remained the official Latin version. Even Father Roothaan published it along with his own literal translation.

72

"**Age, condition of health, and physical constitution,**" *edad, disposición y temperatura.* Cf. Calveras *op. cit., ad loc. Temperatura* is for *temperamento,* and has been translated *physical constitution,* following Feder and Nonell. Cf. Note on no. 205, where the same expression occurs.

73

"Additional Directions," *addiciones.* Here, as in no. 27, *Additional Directions* is used instead of the traditional *additions.* It expresses what they are, as their purpose, stated by St. Ignatius in the title, clearly tells us. This translation is clearer and avoids the use of the word *addition* in a sense not current in English.

82

"Penance." The heading *penance* has been put over this Additional Direction to give it prominence and make it easy to find.

86

"The More Suitable and Safe Form of Penance." The first words of this note have been capitalized to give it prominence. In the Autograph it is distinguished by the word *Note* on the margin. This has been dropped because it leads to confusion with the set of notes that follow. Immediately after this follows *Note I.*

87

"Notes." This heading has been added for clearness. In a set of notes of this kind, the Autograph has no heading but merely *Nota,* with the number on the margin before each one.

91

"The Kingdom of Christ." This title of the Exercise is not in the Autograph, but is used in the Vulgate, which was known to St. Ignatius and presented to the Holy See for approval. The title is also in the Directory, which was begun in the lifetime of St. Ignatius, and drawn up on an outline made by him. On this point see *Monumenta Historica, op. cit.,* p. 306, and the publication of Father Pierre Bouvier, *Directoire Composé par St. Ignace,* Paris, 1917, on the original Directory of St. Ignatius.

The Vulgate also places *Second Week* at the head of this Exercise. We cannot follow in this, since it introduces an inconsistency into the Exercises. The meditation on the Kingdom was intended as an Exercise for the day intervening between the First and Second Weeks, as the note in no. 99 clearly shows. To put *Second Week* over it would make the heading in no. 101 false. That reads "First Day and First Exercise," although another day and another exercise have preceded if we put the heading *Second Week* over the Kingdom.

92

"First Part." This heading has been added for clearness and uniformity. St. Ignatius indicated the second part but not the first.

95

"His summons goes forth. . . . He addresses the words." For the way of translating by separating the two verbs and applying them to separate objects cf. Calveras, *op. cit.,* p. 29.

98

"The offering of myself," *mi oblación.* Since the emphasis is on *my offering,* I have chosen the more emphatic form.

"State and way of life," *vida y estado.* I do not think that this should be translated, as is done at times, as a hendiadys, a *state of life.* The two should be kept on a par. The *state* refers to a vocation that cannot be changed, and the *life* to a manner of living in our vocation. Cf. Introduction to Consideration of Different States of Life, no. 135 with note. The expression is equivalent to the longer one used in no. 15, *estado o modo de vivir.* Neither can it be objected that the *or* between the two members makes them the same. The context shows it does not. Cf. Calveras, *op. cit., ad loc.*

101

"Second Week." This heading is placed before this Exercise for clearness. In the Autograph such headings occur only along the top of the page, here and for the rest of the Week. In the Vulgate and traditionally it is placed over the Kingdom of Christ. This is certainly not the mind of St. Ignatius, as no. 101 begins with the words: "First Exercise and First Contemplation."

109

"According to the light I have received," *según que en si sintiere.* As mentioned before in the note on no. 2, the forms and derivatives of the verb *sentir* commonly have a strong intellectual meaning, and rarely a pure sense signification.

124

"Smell the infinite fragrance and taste the infinite sweetness." For the method of translating by separating the verbs and the objects, cf. *Calveras, op. cit.,* p. 29.

127

"Notes." The heading has been added for clearness. The Autograph as usual has only *First Note, Second Note,* etc., on the margin.

129

"Application of the Senses," *el traer de los sentidos.* The traditional expression, Application of the Senses, taken from the Vulgate Version, has been almost universally adopted in this translation, although St. Ignatius expresses the same thought in different ways. In no. 132, it is *el traer los cinco sentidos.* In no. 123, it is simply *traer los sentidos,* etc.

"Different states of life," *estados.* It is evident from the discussion that follows that St. Ignatius has in mind in this document primarily a state of life, a vocation, and not how I should live, or a way of life in a vocation already chosen.

Different and *of life* are due to the English way of speaking and add nothing to the original.

"In what kind of life or in what state," *en qué vida o estado.* I do not consider *vida* and *estado* as synonyms despite the *or.* Hence I have translated them by "kind of life or state." For confirmation of this translation of *vida,* cf. Nonell, Los Ejercicios, p. 211, and the note on no. 98.

"First Part," " The Standard of Satan." These headings are wanting in the manuscripts, but have been added for clearness. The same holds for the second part, no. 143.

"Three Classes of Men." This heading in the Autograph occurs along the top of the page. It has been placed over the section for convenience and clearness.

Classes, the word used by the Vulgate, and as an alternative by Father Roothaan, has been preferred to pairs, though the latter is more concrete and easy to represent in the imagination.

"Find peace in God our Lord," *hallar en paz a Dios.* Feder interprets these words in this way. Cf. also Calveras, *op. cit., ad loc.*; Longridge, *ad loc.*

153

"Assure their salvation," *saberse salvar.* Father Roothaan and most translators after him have taken the first and most literal meaning of the verb *saber, to know,* and translate, "to know to save themselves." This does not fit the context. It is not a question of knowing how to save themselves, but of using the proper means. Hence, it is rather one of the many idiomatic meanings of the reflexive *saberse* that should be used. Cf. Father Feder's translation, *ad loc.*

155

"As if every attachment had been broken," *que todo lo dexa en affecto.* Cf. Calveras, *op. cit., ad loc.,* and *Monumenta Historica, op. cit.,* p. 360. Father Roothaan thought that *en affecto* might be a copyist's error for *en effecto.* However, all manuscripts have the former and it affords an excellent meaning as the authors cited show.

157

"Attachment opposed to . . . or repugnance to it," *affecto o repugnancia contra la pobreza.* For the manner of translating, cf. Calveras, *op. cit.,* p. 30, and Nonell, *op. cit.,* p. 282.

159

"Notes." The heading has been added for clearness. The Autograph as usual merely indicates the individual notes on the margin. The same holds for no. 162.

163

"Choice of a way of life," *las elecciones.* Cf. note on no. 169 for a discussion of this translation.

165

"Three Kinds of Humility," *tres maneras de humildad.* This title, occurring along the top of the page in the Autograph, has been placed over the section to make this important matter, hidden away in this note, stand out better.

The term *kinds of humility* has been used because it fits well the meaning and corresponds to the Spanish word *maneras.* The word *degree* so often used is not accurate, since the three kinds actually involve five degrees as has been well pointed out by Nonell, *op. cit.,* in discussing this matter. Father Roothaan and the Vulgate use *modi,* and many translators use *mode.* I have preferred *kind* as clearer and more accurate.

"Consent to violate," *sea en deliberar de quebrantar.* Cf. the excellent discussion in Nonell, *Estudio,* p. 194, on the meaning of the Spanish verb *deliberar* in the Exercises. It never means to weigh reasons for and against. Hence, the traditional translation, "to enter into deliberation about breaking," is simply an error in translation. This has been due to the peculiarities of the language of St. Ignatius which had not been investigated at the time of the translations. The same error occurs in no. 166. Cf. also *Monumenta Historica, op. cit.,* p. 190; and Calveras, *ad loc. Deliberar* simply means to choose, decide, consent.

166

"Besides this indifference," *y con esto.* The meaning of this adverbial phrase has been strongly emphasized in the translation because of the common error that has entered many versions. The traditional translations put the two things mentioned in this kind of humility on a par, as though they were two ways of saying the same thing. St. Ignatius says that for this kind of humility, besides indifference, something more is necessary. Cf. the discussion on the point in Nonell, *op. cit., ad loc.,* p. 327ff; and also in the *Authentic Interpretation of the Foundation,* Bouvier, mimeographed translation, West Baden, p. 21.

169

"Choice of a way of life," *elección. Eligir* and *elección* simply mean *to choose* and *a choice.* There is no reason whatever for inventing a new word, or for putting a meaning not in current use on an old word. If we say *election,* to be consistent we should say *elect* for *choose,* which is not done. If the language of the Exercises is properly understood, we find that the word *elección* is expressed in several ways. St. Ignatius in treating this matter uses *determinación, deliberación,* and the verbs *deliberar, determinar,* all in the same sense. Cf. Nonell, *Estudio,* on these words in the *Vocabulario.* The difficulty seems to arise from the fact that St. Ignatius uses the word for a special kind of choice, namely, of a way of life. Hence, to eliminate the difficulty we must add *of a way of life* in English. Just as in Spanish the Saint says *estado* for *state of life,* so he says *elección* for *choice of a way of life.* I have added *way of life* and not *state,* because *way* is wider, and allows both for *state* and the *manner of living in the state.*

Frequently we can leave out *way of life* and simply say *choice* after the title, since St. Ignatius himself is often thinking of rules for any kind of choice, not merely of a choice of a way of life.

Allison Peers, who knows sixteenth-century Spanish and modern English, in speaking of the Exercises translates *elección* by *choice.* Then, because of the traditional rendering, adds in parentheses "or election as it is usually called." Cf. *Studies of Spanish Mystics,* London, 1927, vol. 1, p. 13.

170

"Matters About Which a Choice Should Be Made." This is a part of the heading of the Autograph put above the section for clearness.

179

"I must be indifferent," *hallar me indifferente.* This is an illustration of one of the many cases to which attention has been called. The Spanish does not mean to find oneself indifferent but to be indifferent. The same idiom occurs at the end of this section in "to be at equilibrium."

182

"Come to a decision," *hace deliberación*. This is an illustration of the use of *deliberación* in the sense of *decision* as mentioned above in note no. 165 and elsewhere. It also illustrates the use of the *deliberación* for *elección* mentioned in no. 169. To translate *deliberation* here, as was commonly done, is an error due to the fact that the language of St. Ignatius had not been investigated. Father Feder translates correctly in German, *Entscheidung*.

183

"Choice or decision," *elección o deliberación*. Here we have clear evidence that St. Ignatius uses these two words in the same sense, and of what they mean.

186

"Make my decision," *haga mi determinación*. Here we have an illustration of the use of *determinación* as a synonym for *elección*. Cf. Nonell, *Estudio,* p. 195; and the previous notes on nos. 21, 183, 182, 169.

187

"Consider myself as standing in the presence of my judge," *considerando cómo me hallaré el día del juicio*. Failure to recognize the idiomatic *hallarse* has led to odd translations, "considering what I shall find myself on the day of judgment." Feder interprets correctly.

"Reflect what decision," *pensar cómo querría haber deliberado*. Here the Saint uses the verb *deliberar* in the sense to make a choice.

189

"One's way of living in his state of life," *vida y estado*. *Vida* is often used for way of life, and *estado* for state of life. Cf. note on no. 98 and on 135.

190

"Third Week." This heading appears in the Autograph only at the top of the page. It is put before the Exercises of this Week for clearness.

199

"Talk over motives," *razonar.* Cf. note of Spanish-Latin text on Father Roothaan's translation. The wording adopted is an attempt to bring out the conversation and the reasoning connoted by the word. Cf. note on no. 61, where it is translated, "pour out our thoughts."

"According to circumstances," *según la subiecta materia.* This expression usually refers to the subject matter of the meditation or contemplation, but at times refers to the condition and circumstances of the one meditating. Cf. Nonell, *Estudio,* p. 203. Cf. also Feder, who interprets correctly, *nach den jeweilichen Umstaenden.*

"Meditation on Two Standards," *meditación de los dos binarios.* There is evidently a copyist's error here in the Spanish, since there are three and not two Classes. Whether the passage be corrected to read Two Standards or Three Classes, the mind of St. Ignatius would be equally expressed. Two Standards seems more in harmony with the last sentence. The Saint would hardly repeat the name of the meditation if he meant the same one above. But we have the authority of the Vulgate for Three Classes.

205

"Age, health, and physical constitution," *edad, disposición, y temperatura.* Feder's interpretation of *disposición* as meaning health, and of *temperatura* as meaning physical constitution has been followed. *Temperatura* seems to be for *temperamento.* Cf. Calveras, *ad loc.* In other cases, too, the context shows that St. Ignatius does not mean attitude of mind but condition of health by *disposición.* Cf. no. 72.

208

On the seventh day St. Ignatius says that a repetition of the whole passion is to be made. He uses the expression *junta,* together, at one time. It causes difficulty in getting a clear sentence each time it is used. To prevent an ambiguous statement the passage has been modified to read, "at one exercise and again in the morning."

210

"Rules with Regard to Eating." This heading occurs along the top of the page in the Autograph. The sets of rules in the Exercises are without short titles, but are introduced by a sentence explaining their purpose.

"To secure . . . due order in the use of food," *ordinarse en el comer. Ordinarse* is much stronger than *regulate* or *order oneself.* Hence the longer form has been chosen.

212

"As to foods," *acerca de los manjares. Foods* in the plural seems to indicate sufficiently the meaning of St. Ignatius. As the end of the rule clearly shows, it is not ordinary food that is referred to but delicacies.

214

"How He looks," *cómo mira.* The Spanish refers to the modest reserve with which Christ looks about. Hence the translation of Father Roothaan, *quomodo respiciat,* and Feder's *wie er um sich blickt.* The traditional translation ultimately comes to the same thing, and avoids the connotation of *looks about* or an awkward circumlocution.

218

"Fourth Week." This heading has been placed before the Week. In the Autograph, as in all the Weeks, it is placed at the head of the page.

"No. 299." Though St. Ignatius refers to this mystery in the series of Mysteries of the Life of our Lord, there is nothing in the section to which he refers but a title and a short defense of the apparition of our Lord to Mary. The points must be taken from the First Prelude. Cf. note on no. 299.

225

"As circumstances suggest," *según subiecta materia.* Note that here the phrase *subiecta materia* is used in the wider sense mentioned in the note to no. 199.

230

"Manifest itself in deeds," *se debe poner en las obras.* Roothaan and practically all translators after him have interpreted *ponerse* as passive and translated, "Must be placed in deeds." This gives an exceedingly vague meaning. The reason seems to be because *ponerse* should be translated reflexively. The uses of the reflexive *ponerse* are highly idiomatic. *Ponerse en razón* means simply to be reasonable. So *ponerse en las obras* would mean to be active. Hence, the sentence should read, "love must be active," that is, expresses itself in deeds, must be a love of deeds and not merely words. Longridge translates correctly, "Love must manifest itself in deeds."

238

"The First Method of Prayer." This heading has been inserted for clearness. The portion of the Autograph that follows immediately after the title, *Three Methods of Prayer,* has been dropped down as the heading for no. 239 to which it refers. The present section is a general introduction to this method of prayer.

"**By which the soul may prepare itself,**" *cómo el ánima se apareje . . . en ellos.* We have followed the translation suggested by two older Latin MSS. Cf. Calveras, *op. cit., ad loc.* Both Father Roothaan by the parenthetical completion, *ad facienda exercitia,* and Father Feder by *auf die eigentlichen geistlichen Uebungen,* suggest that the practices prepare for the Exercises of St. Ignatius, properly so called. This can be understood if we remember that in the eighteenth Introductory Observation St. Ignatius suggests these forms of prayer for those not fit for the Exercises proper. Meschler and Oraá in their commentaries suggest the interpretation "prepare for prayer properly so called." A little thought will show that either interpretation would ultimately come to mean a better preparation for the Exercises of St. Ignatius proper.

239

"**I. On the Commandments.**" This heading has been brought down from above as mentioned, and makes the arrangement uniform with the other sections.

Throughout the Methods of Prayer the headings *Additional Direction, Preparatory Prayer, Method,* and *Colloquy* have been added where missing in the Autograph to keep uniformity of arrangement.

242

"**Note I.**" This is missing in the Autograph. We know it should be there from the following Note II.

244

"**Capital Sins,**" *peccados mortales.* Formerly the name *Deadly Sins* was in common use. We now prefer the name *Capital Sins.*

258

"**A measured rhythmical recitation,**" *por compas.* This circumlocution for the Spanish is suggested by Father Roothaan.

261

"Quotation marks," *parénthesis.* Quotation marks have been sub-stituted for the parentheses of the Autograph. The quotations are from The Westminster Version of the Sacred Scriptures, except in two cases where the Spanish text of the Vulgate is quite different.

271

The Vulgate has been followed in giving three points since it seems evident that there is a copyist's error. The quotation from Scripture has no reference to the First Point. Cf. *Monumenta Historica, op. cit.,* p. 460, note.

292

Where the Autograph has no Scripture references they have been inserted from Roothaan here and in no. 294. Additional references were inserted to St. Matthew, St. Mark, and St. Luke in no. 297.

297

The Autograph says, "They gave Him gall and vinegar to drink." The word *gall* has evidently crept in by error. It has been omit-ted. The Vulgate has also omitted the word.

299

The heading mentions two subjects not connected by *and.* There are no points at all. The heading *First Point* was written and then there follows nothing but the defense of the apparition of our Lord to His Blessed Mother. Judging from the material in the First Pre-lude in no. 219, the apparition to our Lady would be the third point if any were given. What the three points would be may be gathered from the history given in no. 219. Cf. F. Hummelauer, *Medita-tionum et Contemplationum Sancti Ignatii de Loyola Puncta,* Freiburg, 1909, *ad loc.*

306

The Autograph says, "He gave them broiled fish and honeycomb." The latter has evidently crept in by error from the mystery recorded in St. Luke 24, 42. The account in St. John mentions bread, and this is what we find in the Vulgate, the Literal Version, and the Spanish MSS of Nadal and Domenech.

311

The three paragraphs are apparently three points and the last part is at the same time a sort of consideration of the whole glorious life as we have at the end of the passion. Cf. *Monumenta Historica, op. cit.,* p. 508; and Hummelauer, *op. cit.,* p. 495f. The punctuation of the Vulgate has been followed.

313

"Rules for Discernment of Spirits. I." This traditional heading has been added to facilitate understanding and use.

For the way of translating by separating the two verbs, *understanding* and *recognizing,* and joining them with separate objects, cf. Calveras, *op. cit., ad loc.,* and p. 29.

315

"To harass with anxiety." The figure of the original, *morder, to bite,* has been interpreted. Cf. Feder, *ad loc.*

320

"Overflowing love," *crecido amor.* The adjective *crecido* has been expressed in different ways to suit the context. Cf. Nonell, *Estudio,* p. 190; and Roothaan in note on Second Prelude to First Exercise; and our note to no. 55.

322

The impersonal form, *por probarnos, to try us,* and similar expressions in this rule evidently suppose God as the subject and it has been so translated: "Because God wishes to try us."

"Build on the property of another," *en cosa ajena pongamos nido.* This aphoristic saying seems to be sufficiently clear by slightly modifying it and putting it in a form more easily understood in English. Roothaan, believing that the correct reading was *en casa,* has changed it to "in the house of another."

325

"He is a weakling before a show of force and a tyrant if he has his own will," *en ser flaco por fuerza y fuerte de grado.* We have tried to make the aphorism clear but have lost in brevity. We might retain the brevity by saying, "Weak perforce and strong by choice." But this would not be very clear. It means that Satan is of necessity weak if we courageously resist, but would gladly tyrannize over us if we give him his way. Cf. Calveras, *ad loc.*

"Shows he is determined and fearless," *muestra mucho rostro.* This might be translated, "If he shows a bold face." We have preferred to interpret the figure.

"Surge up," *es muy crescida.* Another attempt to render the connotation in the *crescido.* At the close of this rule it is rendered by *consummate.*

328

"Rules for Discernment of Spirits. II." This heading has been added to facilitate use.

"Further rules . . . produced in the soul." Instead of saying with the Autograph "for the same effect," the purpose has been repeated as given in the title of the first set of rules.

332

"Suggesting thoughts that are suited," *entrar con la ánima devota.*
The translation given is suggested by the editor of the Spanish-Latin edition, p. 303.

334

"By the trail of Evil," *de su cola serpentina.* Literally, "by his serpent's tail." The translation is an attempt to substitute another figure for one not easily understood in English. However, the scriptural connotation is lost.

336

"Reasoning on the relations," *su proprio discurso de habitudines.* The interpretation of the editor of the Vol. on the Exercises in the *Mon. Hist.* has been followed. Cf. note, p. 534. Roothaan and translators generally have rendered *habitudines* by habits, which in the context does not give a clear meaning. In modern Spanish the word *habitudo* certainly means habit, but in older Spanish words are often closer to the Latin, and this is true of St. Ignatius. In fact the Latin plural of the word is kept here. The only translation that has *relations* that has been examined is Feder. He has *Beziehungen.*

For the way of translating by separating the two verbs *consider* and *distinguish,* and joining them to separate objects, cf. Calveras, *op. cit., ad loc.,* and p. 29.

Similarly, *relations of our concepts* and *consequences of our judgments* have been separated. Cf. Calveras, *op cit., ad loc.,* and p. 29.

337

"Rules for Distribution of Alms." This heading has been inserted for convenience.

"In the ministry of distributing alms." The word *ministry* has been retained in the title to preserve the connotation of the original, namely, that the distribution of alms is a part of the Sacred Ministry especially for those who live according to their office on benefices, the goods of God. Unfortunately this also preserves the unfavorable connotations of the word in English.

339

"Judge would be for the glory of God," *juzgo seer tal.* The word *tal* has been explained in the translation according to Calveras, *op. cit., ad loc.*

345

"Some Notes on Scruples." The heading has been added for clearness. It has been judged better to keep the term St. Ignatius uses, *notes,* and not the usual *rules.* They are exactly what he calls them.

348

"To the spiritual life," *a espirituales exercicios.* Since the article is wanting, it seems evident that exercises of the spiritual life are referred to and not the Exercises. Hence the translation adopted. Cf. Calveras, *op. cit., ad loc.*

349

"Paid some heed to venial sin," *algún caso hacía.* Venial sin is evidently understood here, and has been inserted. Cf. *Mon. Hist.,* Vol. on Ex., p. 546, *ad loc*; and Calveras, *op. cit., ad loc.*

352

"Rules for thinking with the Church." This heading has been added for clearness and is traditional.

"To foster the true attitude of mind," *para el sentido verdadero. To foster* is sufficiently in *para. Attitude of mind* is in *sentido verdadero.* This has been suggested by Feder, *"rechte Gesinnung hegen."* The heading and the usual translations are from the Latin of Roothaan, *"Ad sentiendum vere."*

360

"Praise the building and adornment of Churches," *alabar ornamentos y edificios.* The Vulgate has been followed and *building* put first. This makes *adornment* necessarily refer to churches. There is just a possibility that the Spanish *ornamentos* refers to sacred vestments. The Vulgate seems to solve the problem.

SUGGESTIONS FOR
FURTHER READING

BRODERICK, JAMES, S.J. *Saint Ignatius Loyola: The Pilgrim Years 1491–1538.* New York: Farrar, Straus and Cudahy, 1956.

BROU, ALEXANDRE. *The Ignatian Way to God.* Translated by William J. Young, S.J. Milwaukee: Bruce, 1949.

DALMASES, CANDIDO DE. *Ignatius of Loyola: Founder of the Jesuits.* St. Louis: Institute of Jesuit Sources, 1985.

DUDON, PAUL, S.J. *St. Ignatius of Loyola.* Translated by William J. Young, S.J. Milwaukee: Bruce, 1949.

EGAN, HARVEY D. *The Spiritual Exercises and the Ignatian Mystical Horizon.* St. Louis: Institute of Jesuit Sources, 1976.

GANSS, GEORGE E., ed. *Ignatius of Loyola: The Spiritual Exercises and Selected Works.* With a Preface by John W. Padberg. Classics of Western Spirituality. New York: Paulist Press, 1991.

GUIBERT, JOSEPH. *The Jesuits: Their Spiritual Doctrine and Practice: A Historical Study.* 1964. Reprint, St. Louis: Institute of Jesuit Sources, 1972.

MEISSNER, W. W., S.J. *Ignatius of Loyola: The Psychology of a Saint.* New Haven, Conn.: Yale University Press, 1992.

MUNITIZ, JOSEPH A., AND PHILIP ENDEAN, eds. and trans. *Saint Ignatius of Loyola: Personal Writings.* London: Penguin Books, 1996.

O'MALLEY, JOHN W., S.J. *The First Jesuits.* Cambridge, Mass.: Harvard University Press, 1993.

O'MALLEY, JOHN W., ET AL. *Jesuit Spirituality: A New and Future Resource.* Chicago: Loyola University Press, 1990.

PURCELL, MARY. *The First Jesuit: St. Ignatius Loyola (1491–1556).* Chicago: Loyola University Press, 1981.

RAHNER, HUGO. *Ignatius the Theologian.* San Francisco: Ignatius Press, 1990; 1st edn., Herder & Herder, 1967.

————. *The Spirituality of St. Ignatius Loyola. An Account of Its Historical Development.* Translated by Francis John Smith, S.J. Westminster, Md.: Newman, 1953. Chicago: Loyola University Press, 1980.

STANLEY, DAVID. *A Modern Scriptural Approach to the Spiritual Exercises.* Chicago and St. Louis: Institute of Jesuit Sources, 1967; reprinted, 1986.

ALPHABETICAL INDEX

(The numbers refer to paragraphs, not to pages.)

A

Abstinence, as to food and drink, 210–212; to be praised, 211, 359; prepares the soul for divine inspirations, 213; ordained by the Church is to be observed, 229.

Adam, the sin of, 51.

Additional Directions, to be diligently observed, 6, 88, 130, 207; for Particular Examination of Conscience, 27–30; why the term *Additional Directions* is used for the traditional term *Additions,* note 73; for the First Week, 73–86; for the Second Week, 130; modification of the second Additional Direction, 131; for the Third Week, 206–207; for the Fourth Week, 229.

Affections, v. attachments; those to be cultivated in each Week, 74, 130, 206, 229; to be tested, 342.

Alms, rules for distribution of, 337–344.

Amendment of one's life, directions for, 189.

Angels, v. Satan; sin of the angels, 50.

Annotations, v. Introductory Observations.

Anxiety in prayer to be avoided, 76.

Application of senses, v. senses.

Attachments, purpose of the Exercises to rid ourselves of inordinate, 1, 21; reason for use of term instead of affections, note 1; how to conquer, 16, 155, 157; many want God to come to their inordinate, 169; a vocation from God is without inordinate, 172; what should be done if choice was made because of, 172; must be without inordinate attachments to choose correctly, 179.

Augustine, St., 344.

B

Bernard, St., on vainglory, 351.
Bonaventure, St., 363.
Bread, abstinence from, 210, 211.
Business career not object of vow, 357.

C

Candles lighted in churches, 358.
Carthage, Third Council of, 344.
Choice, of a way of life or state, not to be given to those of little abil-
    ity, 18, note 18; prepared for by meditation on life of Christ,
    135; when treatment of this matter is to begin, 163; why choice
    is used instead of election, note 169, note 183; introduction to,
    169; mutable and immutable choice, 171; about what choice
    may be made, 170–174; how to correct one not rightly made,
    172, 174; three times for making a choice, 175–178; first way of
    making, 178–183; second way of making, 184–188; v. Life.
Christ, calls and wants all under His standard, 137; standard of,
    143–147; to be imitated in manner of eating, 214; what he must
    do who wishes to imitate, in use of the senses, 248; we are the
    better and more secure the more we imitate, 344.
Church, building and adornment of, to be praised, 360.
Church, the, rules for thinking with, 352-370; precepts of, to be
    praised, 361; submission to, 365; governed by the Holy Spirit,
    365.
Circumcision, Meditation on, 266.
Classes, meditation on three, 148–157.
Colloquy, greater reverence in, 3; how to make, 54, 199.
Commandments, Ten, subject matter for examination on deeds, 42;
    the first state, that of observing the, 135; First Method of Prayer
    on, 238–243.
Commandments, of Church, to be praised, 361.
Communion, frequent, 18, 354; at the end of First Week, 44.
Comparison of saints with the living to be avoided, 364.
Composition of place, v. representation, mental.
Confession, general confession in First Week recommended, 44;
    frequent confession to be praised and recommended, 44, 354.

Conscience, the good spirit rouses remorse of, in sinner, 314; the evil spirit afflicts those progressing with anxiety of, 315, 347; the devil seeks to make delicate conscience extreme, 349, 350; v. Examination.

Consolation, exercitant to be questioned when he experiences none, 6; must prepare for coming consolation in desolation, 7; renders meditation easy, 13; will of God may be recognized from it, 175, 176; what it is, 316; we are moved by the good spirit in consolation, 318.

Contemplation, consists in considering things as present, 114.

Contempt, 146.

Continency, to be praised more than matrimony, 356.

Creation, blessing of, to be considered, 234.

Creatures, avengers of offense against their Creator, 60.

D

Damascus, 51.

Death, meditations on, may be added, 71; consideration of, in making choice, 186; consideration of, in distributing alms, 340.

Deceits of the devil, pray that we may know them, 139; the devil does not want deceits to be revealed, 326; how to guard against ordinary, 334.

Decision, 21, as translation of *determinación,* note 21; as meaning of *deliberación,* note 182, note 183.

Deeds, examination of, 42; love manifests itself rather in deeds, 230.

Defect, Particular Examination against particular defect, 24–31; sin of revealing the defects of another, 41; v. faults.

Deliberate, deliberation, not a translation of *deliberación, deliberar,* note 165, note 182, note 183, note 187.

Desolation, what to do if none is experienced, 6; how to deal with exercitant in, 7; meditation difficult in time of, 13; use of, in making choice, 176; description of, 317; how to act in, 319–321; causes of, 322.

Determination, determine, not translation of *determinar, determinación,* note 21, note 169.

Detraction, 41.

E

H

Hell, meditation on, 65–71.

Honor, temptation of the evil one, second step leading to destruction, 142.

Hope, the virtue of, grows in consolation, 316; apparent absence of, in desolation, 317.

Humility, three kinds of, 164–168; kinds not degrees, note 165; consideration of three kinds a preparation for choice of a way of life, 164; the third kind to be sought in colloquies after contemplations, 168.

Hymns, singing of hymns to be praised, 355.

I

Illuminative way, v. way.

Images, to be praised and venerated for the subject they represent, 360.

Imitation of Christ, v. Christ, and also Following of Christ.

Incarnation, Meditation on, 101–109, 262.

Indifference, 23; discussion of term, note 23; of the Third Class, 155; of Second Kind of Humility, 166; necessary disposition for choice of a way of life, 179.

Indulgences, to be praised, 358; v. indults.

Indults, crusade, to be praised, 358.

Intention, must be pure for choice of a way of life, 169.

Introductory observations, 120; discussion of term, note 1.

J

Jubilees, should be praised, 358.

Judgment, day of, exercises on judgment may be given, note at end of, 71; consider what I would like to have chosen on, 187; consider how I would wish to have distributed alms on, 341.

K

Kingdom of Christ, meditation on, 91–99; use of the term *Kingdom of Christ,* note 91.

L

Laughter, not to laugh or cause laughter, 80.

Lazarus, raising of, 161; at the banquet in Simon's house, 285.

Lent, fast and abstinence of, to be praised, 359.

Light, use of the light of day in different weeks, 79, 130, 229.

Love, carnal, those who wish to do more will act against, 97; neglect penance because of, 89.

Love of God, because of faults we forget the love of God, 65; must lead to choice of way of life, 184; in what does true love consist, 230–231; Contemplation to Attain Love, 232–237; must motivate almsgiving, 338; relation of filial fear to love, 370.

Lucifer, v. Satan.

M

Magdalene, conversion of, 282; at resuscitation of Lazarus, 285; anoints Jesus at the supper in the house of Simon, 286; Jesus appears to, 300.

Magi come to adore the child, 162, 267.

Magnanimity, exercitant to enter retreat with, 5.

Man, why created, 23.

Martha, sister of Lazarus, 285.

Mary, Blessed Virgin, Mother of God, colloquy to, 63, 147; at the Annunciation, 102–108; desolation of, 208; to imitate in the use of the senses, 248; farewell to her Son, 273.

Mary Magdalene, v. Magdalene.

Mass, exercitant should be free to attend each day, 20; praise frequent hearing of, 355.

Matrimony, not to be praised as much as virginity, 356.

Matthew, St., his call to be an Apostle, 175.

Memory, use in meditation, 50–52.

Mercy, works of, to be explained to uneducated exercitant, 18; Colloquy of, 61, 71.

Mysteries of the life of our Lord, 262–312.

N

Nativity, contemplation on, 110, 264.

Note, meaning of term in Exercises and way of indicating them, note 31, note 49.

O

Oaths, 38-40.

Obedience due to Church, 353, 365.

Orders of superiors must be upheld, 362.

P

Palm Sunday, 4, 161, 287.

Particular examination of conscience, v. examination.

Passion, matter for the Third Week, 4; how to contemplate, 190–198, 200–209; repetition of the whole passion in one day, 208; 7th day, 209.

Patience, to be practiced in desolation, 321.

Paul, St., his call to be an Apostle, 175; Christ appears to him, 311.

Penance, kinds of, and fruits of, 82–89; in Second Week, 130; in Fourth Week, 229; more should be done in time of desolation, 319; praise both exterior and interior, 359.

Perfection, outside the Exercises we may urge those fit to every form of perfection, 15; how we are to attain it in whatever vocation God gives us, 135; we must seek it in a choice well made, 173; rule for practicing it, 185, 339; how to make progress in it, 189; praise works conducive to perfection, 357.

Perseverance in prayer, 12, 13.

Peter, St., in the garden, 201, 290, 291; called three times, 275; walks upon the waters, 280; at the Transfiguration, 284; Christ washes his feet, 289; denies Christ, 291, 292; comes to the sepulcher and sees Christ, 302; receives primacy, 306.

Petition, made in prelude before meditation, in First Week, 48, 55, 65; in Second Week, 91, 104, 139, 152; in Third Week, 193, 203; in Fourth Week, 221; in Contemplation to Attain Love, 233.

Presence of God, place yourself in the presence of God before prayer, 75, 239; God dwells in creatures in many ways, 235; God present in creatures by essence, power, and presence, 39.

Presupposition, 22; note on this heading, note 22.

Pride, cause of the fall of the angels, 50; third step in Satan's plan for our ruin, 142; cause of desolation, 322.

Principle, first principle and foundation, 23; why first is added, note 23.

Progress, the Exercises should be given according to the progress of the exercitant, 17; way to progress, 189 near end.

Promise, director should warn against rash promises, 14; should not advise promises during retreat, 15.

Proposition, v. statement.

Psalmody, to be praised, 355.

Purgative way, v. way.

R

Reading, passages from the Gospel, Following of Christ, Lives of Saints during Second and subsequent Weeks, 100; only the mystery about to be contemplated should be read, 127.

Reformation of one's life, 189.

Relics to be praised and reverenced, 358.

Religious life, caution about rashly making promise to enter, 14; the director must not urge the exercitant to religious life, 15; praise religious life, 356; must praise vows of religion, 357.

Repetitions, how to make them, 62, 118, 119.

Representation, mental, of the place, how it is made, 47; discussion of term adopted, note 47.

Repugnance, what to do when there is a repugnance to poverty, 157.

Reverence, greater reverence required in acts of the will, 3; the reverence required in oaths, 38, 39; act of reverence to God at beginning of prayer, 75.

Riches, should not be preferred to poverty, 23; desire of, snare of Satan, 142; what to do when one is not indifferent to, 157; second kind of humility is indifferent to riches, 166; third kind of humility chooses poverty rather than riches, 167; friends share riches, 231.

Rules, for making a good choice, 184–189; with regard to eating, 210–217; for discernment of spirits, 313–336; concerning scruples, 345–351; for distribution of alms, 337–344; for thinking with the Church, 352–370.

S

Saints, lives of, may be read in Second Week and after, 100; may occupy ourselves while eating with the lives of the saints, 215; we must praise the relics of, and pray to the saints, 358.

Satan, his sin and punishment, 50; leader of the enemy, 140; standard of, 140–142.

Scruples, notes on, 345–351.

Seclusion, recommended for the Exercises, 20.

Secret, the devil wishes his temptations to be kept secret, 326.

Senses, the first method of prayer on the five senses to be explained to the uneducated, 18; application of, 65–70, 121–126, 129, 132–134, 204, 208, 209, 226, 227; first method of prayer on five senses, 247–248; to imitate Christ or the Blessed Virgin in the use of, 248.

Shepherds, meditation on, 162, 265.

Sin, venial and mortal sin, 35, 36; exercise on sin, 45–64; method of prayer on Capital Sins, 244, 245.

Singing of hymns and psalms to be praised, 355.

Sleep, recalling exercises before sleep and on waking from sleep, 73, 74; external penance with regard to sleep, 84.

Solitude, recommended for Exercises, 20.

Sorrow for sins, 55–61.

Spirits, rules for discernment of different spirits, 313–336.

Standards, two, meditation on, 136–148; colloquy of, 147, 156, 168.

State of life, v. choice of a way of life, way of life.

Station Churches to be praised, 358.

Steps, to pride and all sin, 142; three steps to humility and all the virtues, 146.

Summary of an exercise, Fourth Exercise of the First Week, 64.

Hail, Holy Queen

Hail, holy Queen, mother of mercy,
our life, our sweetness, and our hope.
To you do we cry,
poor, banished children of Eve.
To you do we send up our sighs,
mourning and weeping in this valley of tears.
Turn then, most gracious advocate,
your eyes of mercy toward us,
and after this our exile
show unto us the blessed fruit of your womb, Jesus.
O clement, O loving, O sweet Virgin Mary.

V. Pray for us, O holy Mother of God.
R. That we may be made worthy of the promises of Christ.

Let us pray.
Almighty and everlasting God, by the cooperation of
the Holy Spirit you prepared the body and soul of Mary,
glorious Virgin and Mother, to become the worthy
habitation of your Son; grant that by her gracious intercession,
in whose commemoration we rejoice, we may be delivered
from present evils and from everlasting death. Through
the same Christ our Lord.
R. Amen.

V. May the divine assistance remain with us always.
R. Amen.

Avery Dulles, S.J., is the Laurence J. McGinley Professor at Fordham University. An internationally known theologian, lecturer, and author, he has written more than 600 articles and nineteen books and has been president of the Catholic Theological Society of America and the American Theological Society. A priest and a convert, he has written, "I still live off what I then discovered [while a seminarian after World War II] about meditation, discernment, obedience, and loyalty, with the help of that great master of Christian prudence, Ignatius of Loyola."

John F. Thornton is a literary agent, former book editor, and the coeditor, with Katharine Washburn, of *Dumbing Down* (1996) and *Tongues of Angels, Tongues of Men: A Book of Sermons* (1999). He lives in New York City.

Susan B. Varenne is a New York City high-school teacher with a strong avocational interest in and wide experience of spiritual literature (M.A., University of Chicago Divinity School; Ph.D., Columbia University).